Alaskan Eskimo Life in the 1890s

As Sketched by Native Artists

George Phebus, Jr.

University of Alaska Press

Faibanks, Alaska

Library of Congress Cataloging-in-Publication Data

Phebus, George E.
    Alaskan Eskimo life in the 1890s as sketched by native artists /
George Phebus, Jr.
       p.   cm.
    Originally published: Washington : Smithsonian Institution Press,
1972.
    Includes bibliographical references.
    ISBN 0-912006-79-X (acid-free paper)
    1. Eskimo art.   2. Eskimos--History--19th century.   3. Eskimos-
-Social life and customs.   I. Title.
E99.E7P46   1995
305.897'10798'0222--dc20   95-19544
                                       CIP

International Standard Book Number: 0-912006-79-X
Library of Congress Card Number: 95-19544

Printed in the United States by BookCrafters, Inc. on recycled acid-free paper.

This publication was printed on acid-free paper which meets the minimum
requirements for American National Standard for Information Sciences—Perma-
nence of Paper for Printed Library Materials, ANSI Z39.48.1984.

Book design by Elizabeth Sur.
Cover design by Dixon Jones, IMPACT Graphics, UAF Rasmuson Library.

Contents

Foreword   This book calls attention to a late-19th-century form of Eskimo art that has received little recognition. In the 1890s the Eskimos of northwestern Alaska, working with materials that were new to them— paper, watercolors, crayons, and pencils supplied by teachers in the newly established government and mission schools—produced remarkably vivid and accurate sketches depicting the arctic terrain and Eskimo activities. It was not a wholly new art form. It was part of a tradition that had its beginnings several centuries earlier in Eskimo pictographs, the last major prehistoric art style of the western arctic.

Pictographic art consisted of small silhouette engravings on ivory that showed such typical Eskimo activities as harpooning whales and walrus, shooting caribou with bow and arrow, driving dog sleds, dancing, wrestling, and racing. These vignettes of Eskimo life were applied most frequently to the long, narrow handles of bow drills or tool bags and were produced only at Bering Strait and the coastal areas immediately adjacent, from Norton Sound north- ward to Kotzebue Sound. Pictographic art had its greatest vogue in the second half of the 19th century, after the arrival of American whaling vessels in1848, but a few examples have been excavated at late prehistoric Eskimo sites at Cape Prince of Wales and Kotzebue Sound, showing that this art form was truly aboriginal.

In the earliest examples the figures were extremely simple. A man would be represented by a single line for the body, other lines for arms and legs, and a dot for the head. Caribou and other game animals were rendered more realistically, with a few lines or hatches to fill out the body. In the late decades of the 19th century the engraved figures became thicker and more rounded out, with dense cross-hatching which, when smeared with the customary charred grease from the seal oil lamp, produced heavily blackened figures that stood out prominently against the ivory background. A more fundamental change, stimulated by the Yankee whalers' scrimshaw and other contemporary illustrations, occurred when Eskimo carvers began to decorate cribbage boards and entire wal- rus tusks with hunting scenes, landscapes, ice floes, and fully rounded figures. Delicate shading indicated land forms, sea ice, and the texture of fur and clothing. These later engravings, showing true perspective, were the ivory equivalents of the spirited sketches and watercolors described by Mr. Phebus in this volume. The more durable—and salable—works in ivory have found their way into museums and private collections, and now are recognized as the final artistic products of a people who had been making sophisti- cated ivory carvings for 2,000 years.

The drawings reproduced here have remained virtually unknown except to a handful of students of Eskimo culture. Of the many such drawings that were produced, only a few have been preserved. That they are known at all is due to the fortunate circumstance that some Alaskan school teachers, recognizing the artistic merit of the sketches, sent a few of them to the former United States Bureau of Education in Washington, which in turn exhibited them at various expositions as examples of the work the bureau was conducting among the Eskimo. With the demise of the Bureau of Education the exhibits were transferred, in 1910, to the Smithsonian Institution. From this collection Mr. Phebus has selected the examples illustrated here.

One point should be made clear. Though produced in Eskimo schools, these drawings are not the work of young school children. The technical proficiency and attention to detail assure us that they are the work of youths or young adults thoroughly familiar with the activities portrayed. The artists knew precisely what was done when a walrus was harpooned and had to be hauled up on the ice, how a huge whale was towed ashore by umiaks, or how a ceremony was performed. The young Eskimo artists concentrated mainly on themes that were central to their traditional way of life, such as hunting caribou, harpooning sea mammals, killing polar bears, driving dog teams, fishing, trapping, bartering. Some scenes portray, in remarkable detail, the elaborate clothing, animal masks, and other paraphernalia worn by participants in ceremonies held in the kashim.

To determine the full meaning of these scenes of Eskimo life by Eskimo artists, Mr. Phebus has made a careful survey of the literature, citing pertinent passages from the works of ethnographers who have described the material culture, hunting practices, and social life of the Eskimos around Bering Strait. The result is a faithful and vivid record of Alaskan Eskimo culture at the end of the 19th century, when it still existed in its native form.

Henry B. Collins
Archeologist Emeritus
Smithsonian Institution

Acknowledgments

Appreciation is expressed to Dr. Clifford Evans, chairman of the Smithsonian's Department of Anthropology, and to Dr. Henry Collins, Smithsonian archeologist emeritus and arctic expert, for their technical assistance and to Dr. William Sturtevant, curator, Division of North American Anthropology, Smithsonian Institution, for his encouragement.

A special debt of gratitude is owed to Betty Meggers, George Metcalf, Bethune Gibson, Frances Ball, and the staff of the Smithsonian's Conservation-Analytical Laboratory, all of whom assisted generously in the preparation of the material.

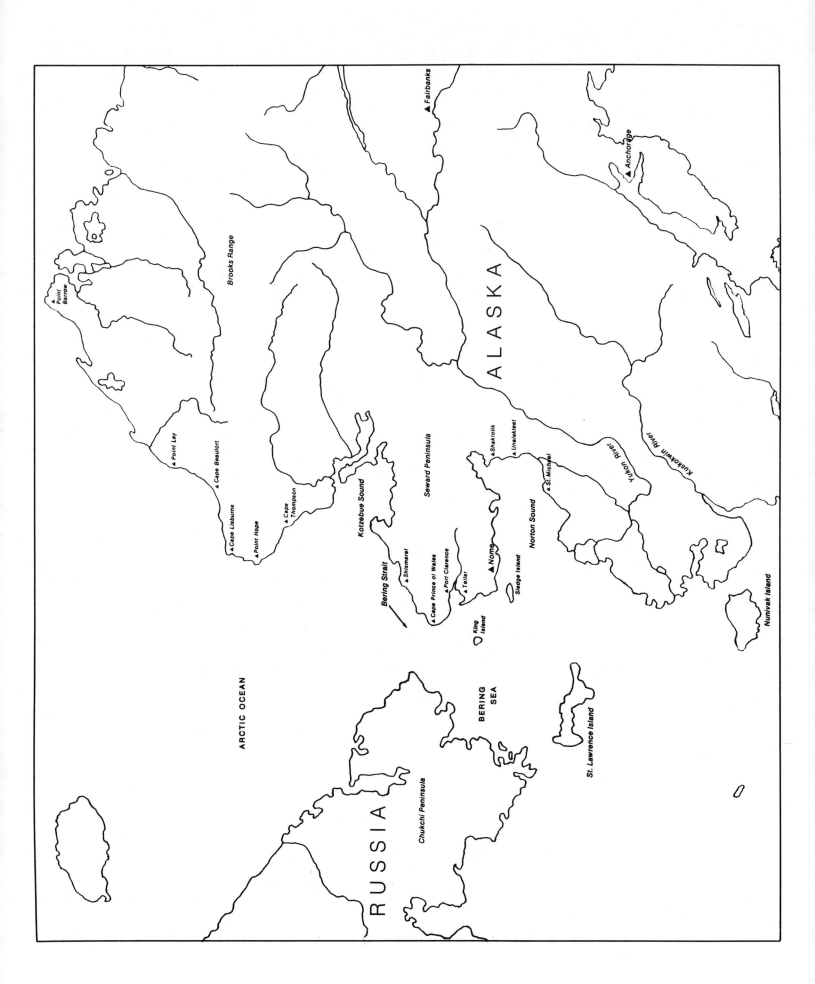

Commentary

In the summer of 1967 a number of drawings and paintings depicting Alaskan Eskimo life in the late 19th century were discovered in an old storage unit in the Smithsonian's Department of Anthropology in the National Museum of Natural History (NMNH). These Eskimo life scenes, in pencil, ink, crayon, and watercolor, were mounted on more than twenty large cardboard posters. Printed captions on these exhibition posters attributed the collection to the old United States Bureau of Education, and each poster was labeled "Education in Alaska." The sketches were similar to mounted artwork used in the printing of plates for early publications of the Smithsonian's Bureau of American Ethnology, and apparently they inadvertently had been stored with such materials.

An exhaustive search resulted in only meager success in accumulating historical and geographical data directly connected with the actual drawing and collecting of these Eskimo sketches. The only written records in the Smithsonian's Department of Anthropology regarding the old Bureau of Education's Alaskan ethnological collection are contained on two accession cards of the United States National Museum (USNM):

> This material was collected by the Bureau of Education of the Interior Department for exhibition at various expositions. The museum of this bureau, which had existed since 1883, being abandoned, the material was transferred to the National Museum in January 1910.[1]

> Drawings. (21) Eskimo. Kotzebue Sound, Alaska. Mounted on boards.[2]

Further research in the Smithsonian's files and archives did not indicate that the illustrations had been exhibited or published following their inclusion in the ethnology collections of the Smithsonian Institution. Many of the early Smithsonian displays, however, had not been photographed, and some of the old file prints and glass negatives had been discarded.

The second catalog card attributes all of the sketches to the region of Kotzebue Sound in northwestern Alaska. One would not argue that Kotzebue Sound could have been the source for some of these illustrations, but hand-lettered captions on other drawings identify different sources. Among such captions the following localities are mentioned: "Teller," near Port Clarence, Seward Peninsula, Norton Sound; "Unalaklik River," east side of Norton Sound; and "Koko Creek," probably near the village of Koko on the lower Yukon River.

Certain other scenes, because of the activity portrayed, the clothing worn, or the equipment depicted, are not attributable to the Kotzebue Sound area. Such discrepancies in the catalog data or provenance are not uncommon, however, in the old records.

While investigating this problem the author examined a number of different specimens from the Bureau of Education's collections.

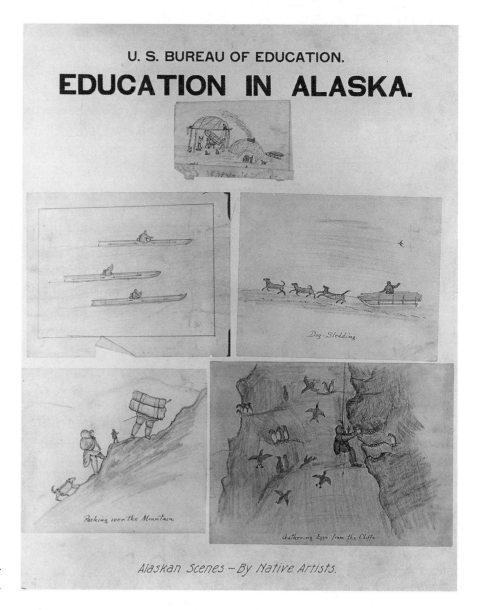

One of the exhibition posters featuring work of Alaskan Eskimo students.

Some of these are of particular interest because they still have their original, detailed identification tags that provide data on their collection.

Two carved, painted wooden spoons have an attached postcard (dated 19 May 1898) that reads: "Indian Spoons, by Shegaluk Boy John. Koserefsky School. Alaska." [3] Koserefsky School was on the left bank of the Yukon, near the mouth of Shageluk slough, and Holy Cross Mission was nearby. A post office was established there in September 1899. [4]

A small, intricately carved wooden box has a penciled inscription, on the underside of the lid, that reads: "The Sloyd School at Teller Alaska." Written in ink on a tag glued to the bottom of the box are the words: "Sloyd [carved] at Norw. Ev. Luth. Synod Mission school. At Teller Reindeer Station Alaska. " [5] Teller was originally established as a reindeer station by the Reverend Sheldon Jackson in 1892 and named after Henry Moore Teller, then Secretary of the Interior. Later the station was moved from its original location on

Grantly Harbor to the north shore of Port Clarence. A post office was established there in 1900.[6] Records of the old Bureau of Education show that Teller Reindeer Station was under the direction of the Norwegian Lutheran Church in 1900.[7]

It was concluded from the above that this collection of Eskimo art was the product of various students in public schools and private mission schools throughout an area of northwestern Alaska under the jurisdiction of the Bureau of Education of the Department of the Interior. As some mission schools were operated in the Kotzebue Sound region during the 1890s, some of the illustrations may be properly attributed to that area.[8]

The Eskimo are recognized as skilled and accomplished artisans, especially in ivory, but little is known of their sketching and painting in the late 19th century. The similarity between certain examples of 19th-century ivory engraving and some of the art in the Bureau of Education collection clearly suggests that the Eskimo artisan could easily adapt to different media without appreciable alteration of style. Various Eskimo artists have created sketches and paintings for the art market, but few such works created in the 19th century have survived.[9]

The Smithsonian collections include examples of Eskimo art that are similar to the drawings illustrated here. Outstanding among such examples are two sketchbooks of Guy Kakarook of St. Michael (Norton Sound) that apparently were produced about 1903.[10] Kakarook's work focuses upon Eskimo activities, nature studies, and scenes along the Yukon River. Other similar specimens include three sketches that depict Canadian Eskimos with members of the Spicer Expedition. These drawings, probably dating from about the 1870s, were collected by Captain John Spicer on Baffin Island in the area of Cumberland Sound. They were entered in the Smithsonian collections in 1894.[11]

Two newspaper clippings in the Smithsonian's archival files also deal with the history of Eskimo graphic art. The earliest, dated 24 October 1909, refers to the "Amazing Talent of an Eskimo Artist."[12] The artist featured in the story was a Canadian Eskimo by the name of Panikpah who apparently resided in the area of Ellesmere Island, Northwest Territories. The reproductions of his work accompanying the article bear a resemblance to the Bureau of Education sketches in quality and execution except that they depict distant scenes rather than intimate views.

A second newspaper account of more recent vintage relates the discovery by artist Rockwell Kent of George Aden Ahugupuk, an Alaskan Eskimo artist.[13] Ahugupuk, residing at Shishmaref on the Seward Peninsula, frequently is mentioned by authors as one of the outstanding contributors to 20th-century Alaskan Eskimo art.

A note in a Bureau of Education report indicates that students were drawing by pencil at the Cape Prince of Wales missionary school in 1891,[14] and some of the sketches in the Smithsonian's collection bear the date 1892. The collections of the Bureau of Education's museum, in Washington, D.C., were assembled principally for exhibit at various national and international exhibitions, such as at Paris in 1900 and at Jamestown in 1903,[15] and the museum was closed in 1908. Consequently, it is likely that most of the sketches were executed between 1890 and 1900; some, however, could have been produced a few years earlier or as much as ten years later. The following selected listing of missionary and public schools in northwestern Alaska [16] indicates likely sources of the drawings in the collection and the approximate dates of their execution:

Missionary schools	Known date of operation
Point Barrow	1889
Point Hope	1889
Kotzebue (Cape Blossom)	1889
Cape Prince of Wales	1889

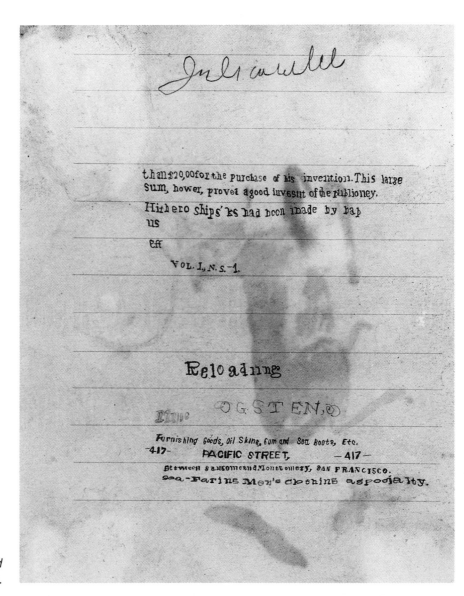

Examples of student lessons found on reverse of drawings.

Unalakleet	1889
Port Clarence	1892
St. Lawrence Island	1894

Public schools	*Known date of operation*
Port Clarence	1892
Cape Prince of Wales	1895
Point Barrow	1896
Teller	1900
Kotzebue	1901
Unalakleet	1902
Wainwright	1904

It is probable that a scarcity of paper in some of the Bureau of Education schools required the teachers and students to economize on this material. Most of the sketches are drawn on the unlined side of school tablet paper, and many of them bear the lessons of the day on the ruled side.

The drawings are grouped here according to similarities of the activities depicted and the relationship between succeeding scenes. An attempt has been made to identify the localities of the various scenes, although in some instances the evidence was scant and the identifications conjectural. Some of the drawings apparently were labeled by the students themselves and others seem to have been titled by teachers. (Herein, such original titles are in boldface type. The author has provided titles for originally unlabeled drawings and in some cases, for descriptive purposes, has added a subtitle to the original. Measurements of the original drawings are given in inches, with height preceding width.)

Since the author is not a specialist in arctic ethnology, he has drawn heavily upon the many detailed narratives and studies available on northwestern Alaska. Accordingly, much of the credit for this study should go to those contributors listed in the notes.

No attempt has been made to judge these drawings in regard to their quality as art. Their greatest value lies in their providing us with a pictorial record of Alaskan Eskimo life as depicted by native artists just prior to the drastic changes of the 20th century.

Eskimo subsistence

Whaling

From Point Barrow south along the arctic coast whaling was a major contributor to the Eskimo economy. The whale supplied life's necessities for the coastal Eskimo much as the buffalo supplied the wherewithal of the Plains Indian. In both cases very little of the beast was left unused. The Eskimo took from the whale the skin, blubber, and meat as food and then used the bone, baleen (fibrous whale tooth), and some of the blubber as raw materials, fuels, or items of trade.

In the spring the bowhead whales migrated north through the Bering Sea. In the fall these whales returned south by a different route, one which took them farther east and away from the Alaskan coast. The spring migration took them near the Alaskan Eskimo villages along the coast from Point Hope to Point Barrow, but in the fall only the natives of Point Barrow had access to them. The whaling season could last for as long as two months, but sometimes bad weather reduced the actual hunting time to only a few weeks. Therefore, the Eskimo could not rely on a minimum number of whales annually. If the whaling season was a poor one, it became necessary to accelerate other subsistence activities, such as sealing, to compensate for the food loss.

The Eskimo concept of religion was essentially animistic. All of the creatures in the Eskimo world were endowed with a spirit, and that spirit was not to be offended. Elaborate purification was ritualized in preparation for the whaling season. All implements related to whaling in any way were carefully cleaned to remove any traces that might have remained from the previous whaling season, for such contamination would surely offend the spirit of the "first" whale and thus cause all other whales to shun the village. To insure the prosperity of the whaling season, certain prescribed regulations were involved in the killing of all whales, but the most elaborate ceremony was reserved for the first whale of the season.

The approach of schools of the dolphin-like beluga signaled that the larger bowhead whales were not far behind. The belugas, themselves, were eagerly sought by the Eskimo, who were able to make large kills in the shallows of Kotzebue Sound after cleverly maneuvering the animals there from deeper water.

As soon as the belugas appeared the Eskimo began to watch the large ice formation offshore, searching for "leads," or separations in the ice, through which the bowheads might appear. When a sighting was made the tough skin boats, called umiaks, were launched, and the hunters—equipped with harpoons, lances, and inflated skin floats—began the chase.

Great caution was taken when approaching the whale, but boat accidents were common and crews were lost, as few Eskimos ever learned to swim. If several boats were involved in the hunt and a kill was made, the crews would combine forces and tow the whale to the edge of the solid ice nearest the village. If the whale was small it was hauled from the water onto the ice; but if it was of average size, or large, the head would be raised out of the water and, eventually, when the bulk had been reduced by preliminary butchering, the remainder could be hoisted onto the ice. Following certain preparations and formalities, the actual butchering began, with the men using keen-edged whaling spades and hooks. Other members of the village assisted throughout the operation.

Following the advent of commercial arctic whaling, about 1848,[17] a major element of the traditional economy of certain Eskimo populations was in jeopardy. As the price for baleen rose from cents to dollars per pound the arctic whaling fleets grew proportionately. Baleen was in great demand in the second half of the 19th century, especially for use in the manufacture of corset stays and buttons; accordingly, by the year 1880 a United States revenue cutter had been assigned to arctic waters to act primarily on behalf of the whalers and secondarily as a "moral barrier" between the whalers and the Eskimos.

During the 1890s with the rapid depletion of the whale population in the arctic and its obvious economic effect on many coastal populations, certain farsighted individuals instituted measures to alleviate the Eskimo's plight. Some land-based commercial whaling companies employed Eskimo crewmen, thereby compensating, somewhat, for the inroads they had been making into the native economy. The most significant aid came with the introduction of the reindeer into Alaska—a program almost solely the result of the labors of the Reverend Sheldon Jackson, general agent for the Bureau of Education in Alaska.

During this period the United States government tried to keep contact between the whalers and the Eskimos to the barest minimum, but even so there was enough contact to create additional hardships for the Eskimo. One ethnologist has commented that "the Eskimo population of northwest Alaska never recovered numerically from the epidemic brought about by diseases introduced from the whaling ships." [18]

A commercial whale might supply 1,500 to 2,000 pounds of baleen plus additional income derived from the rendering of the whale oil as a component for soap and candles. In 1887 the arctic whaling fleet of 32 vessels accumulated 561,694 pounds of baleen.[19] Hypothetically, if there were 1,500 pounds of baleen in an average bowhead whale, then something on the order of 400 whales were destroyed that season, and similar numbers were destroyed in preceeding and succeeding years until the beginning of the 20th century. During the early years of the 20th century the demand for baleen decreased, but the reduced number of whales was insufficient to offset the low market. By 1915 commercial whaling in the arctic had ceased.

1 / Fast Boat　A whaling crew pursues a bowhead whale. Pencil, ink, and crayon; 5x7¾.

This sketch dates from a period following 1888, when certain coastal Eskimo were employed by various commercial whaling companies.[20] The whaleboat is a company craft, and its steersman, wearing a cap, probably represents a company supervisor. The whale, still alive, is held by a single harpoon line, but the forward crewman is about to dispatch it with a whale gun, a rifle that fired an explosive projectile.

2 / Signaling a kill. Pencil, ink and crayon; 4¾x7¾.

The whaleboat's hoisted ensign signifies that a kill has been made. Two company men are in the crew: the steersman, known in Eskimo jargon as the oomalik, and the man who is supervising from his position in the bow.

3 / Towing a Whale   Several crews cooperate in towing a carcass. Pencil, ink, and crayon; 5x8.

Four umiaks proceed with the dead whale in tow. The traditional Eskimo umiak doggedly held its ground against the competition of the wooden-staved commercial whaleboat. The umiak was light, could be handled easily both on the ice and the sea, and was relatively simple to repair. Generally, it was the ideal craft for its purpose. Even the commercial whalers were known to use it.[21]

4 / Cutting In Whale carcass being hauled upon the ice. Pencil, ink, and crayon, 5x8.

The whaling crew pulls the carcass onto the ice by means of a double block-and-tackle system, although the artist has seen fit to depict a rather small whale. In the case of an average-size or large whale the exposing of the head was about all that could be accomplished in the initial stage.

5 / A whale is on the ice and ready for "cutting in." Pencil, ink, and crayon; 4¾x7¾.

This drawing resembles a typical, posed tintype of the 19th century. Two company men are depicted near the tail of the bowhead whale. One of the Eskimo crewmen is wiping his brow as if to say, despite the block and tackle, "It's still hard work!" The long-handle instruments in the right foreground are whaling hooks and spades used in the butchering process.

6 / Killing a beluga from the ice. Pencil, ink, and crayon; 5x7¾.

During the milder months, the beluga occasionally wandered into coastal shallows or, in some cases, were driven there by the Eskimos. Kotzebue Sound was the most noted area for beluga hunting.

The two Eskimos are using modern firearms and a retrieving harpoon, a necessary instrument for recovering a carcass. The dark oval objects with what appear to be straps or handles probably represent equipment bags that contain ammunition and tools.[22] The Eskimo firing the rifle is wearing a bead-type labret commonly worn by males of Kotzebue Sound and other areas of the arctic coast.

Walrus hunting

The walrus played a crucial role in the economy of the Eskimo. It provided materials for umiak covers and whaling rope and an abundant supply of blubber for food and of meat that traditionally was reserved for dogs. In the later years of the 19th century the demand for Eskimo art made the walrus even more important because its tusks were the principal source of ivory. Entire walrus herds were slaughtered for their ivory, just as whales were slaughtered for their baleen.

It was in September that large walrus herds congregated among the fields of slow-moving, broken ice. In that month the Eskimo hunters would attempt to approach the walrus as the animals lay on the drifting ice. The following series of six illustrations mirrors the activities of Eskimo walrus hunters along the coast of the Arctic Ocean or in the Bearing Sea, north of St. Lawrence Island.

7 / Hunting Walrus Hunting walrus amidst floating ice. Pencil, ink, and crayon; 6½ x 8¼ .

The man in the stern is the steersman, who usually was the captain and owner of the boat. The harpoonor stands ready in the bow. A crew of eight usually was the maximum for most umiaks. Position in the boat was important since it was directly related to the division of the carcass following the kill. The importance of position in the boat was even more significant among the whaling crews, but the rules varied somewhat, depending upon whether the crew was following the whaling customs at Point Barrow, for example, or at Point Hope, farther south.[23]

In this scene the artist has demonstrated his familiarity with walrus habits by depicting the young walrus being carried upon the back of the female.

8 / Walrus Hunt   Harpooning a bull walrus. Pencil, ink, and crayon; 9x12.

There is a striking similarity between this drawing and the previous one, and both may be the work of the same artist. In this sketch the Eskimo crew is attired in "gut" frocks, foul-weather gear made from the intestines of walrus or seal. One walrus has been struck and a crew member is about to toss a sealskin float into the water. The float, when attached to the walrus, retarded the movement of the fleeing animal; it also prevented the carcass from sinking. Here, again, the female and young are shown in characteristic position.

Special care was taken when hunting the walrus from the umiak: "It is a very dangerous thing to hold a harpooned walrus from an oomiak [umiak] for the infuriated beast is likely to charge the boat, hook his tusks over the side, and break it in half with a tremendous downward pull." [24]

9 / Walrus Hunt Using a sealskin
float. Pencil and ink; 8x10.

Despite the similarity between this
sketch and the two preceding scenes,
this rendition of walrus hunting is
obviously the work of a different artist.
One walrus is dead and another has
been struck. Probably unintentionally,
the artist has indicated more work
here than the small crew could possibly handle.

10 / Walrus Hunt   Hunting walrus on the ice. Pencil, ink, and crayon; 9x12.

The walrus have been caught asleep on the ice and the Eskimo hunters are shooting and harpooning them as they attempt to gain the partial safety of the sea. Whalebone stakes and retrieving lines have been prepared as aids in retrieving the carcasses of walrus that die in the sea. When the hunters pull on the lines encircling the stakes there is sufficient force to extract a walrus carcass from the sea, or even change the position of a small whale. In effect, the technique is a native-developed pulley system.

In this scene, however, the artist has drawn "the cart before the horse," for it is doubtful that the walrus could have been sleeping so soundly that the placing of the stakes would not have roused them.

11 / Drawing Walrus Ashore Using native block and tackle. Pencil, ink, and crayon; 9x12.

Here, the effectiveness of the Eskimo pulley system is quite evident. A large walrus is being hoisted onto the ice.

In addition to the technical aspects of this scene, the artist has taken pains to indicate certain physical traits of the Eskimo men: the tonsure-type hairstyles and the lip incisions for labrets so characteristic of natives of the northern Bering Sea and Arctic Ocean areas.

12 / Drawing Walrus Ashore   Using
native native block and tackle. Pencil and
ink; 8x8¼.

Like the preceding sketch, this scene
depicts the hauling of walrus carcasses onto the ice; the art style,
however, is more like that of sketch
9. In this instance the whalebone
stakes have eyes through which the
hoisting lines are drawn, and the force
is applied in a slightly different manner.

34

Seal hunting

Sealing along the arctic coasts was a year-round activity, but the greatest variety and the largest number of seals were taken in the winter months on the ice pack at the seals' "breathing holes" or in the "leads" where the ice had parted. Principally, the capture was effected by harpoons, nets, or guns.

Normally, the seal was hunted individually, but in the case of the bearded seal, a considerably larger mammal, communal effort was frequent. The skin of the bearded seal was highly prized for its use as boot soles and umiak covers.

13 / Approaching a ribbon seal.
Pencil, ink, and crayon; 5x7¾.

An Eskimo is propelling his kayak toward a ribbon seal (comparatively
rare and highly prized for its uniquely
patterned fur) that is adrift on a cake
of ice. This scene could represent a
surprise encounter, as the Eskimo appears unprepared to capitalize on his
good fortune. Encounters such as this
would occur in the spring when much
of the ice was free and drifting and
the hunting could be conducted from
boats.

The Eskimo in this illustration may
have been from King Island, as his
kayak fits the description of such boats
from that area.[25] An identical kayak
model in the ethnology collections of
the National Museum of Natural History
is attributed to the Kaviagmut Eskimo
of Cape Nome, an area also frequented
by the King Islanders.[26]

14 / Hauling up a sea lion. Pencil, ink, and crayon; 5x8.

In this summer scene Eskimos are pulling ashore a bearded seal. As in the previous drawing, the kayak suggests that these Eskimos could be from King Island, Sledge Island, or one of the various Eskimo groups on the Kaviak (Seward) Peninsula.

The dome-shaped dwelling in this sketch is called a "tupek." It is quite similar to a dwelling used by the Malamute Eskimo near Cape Espenberg.[27] Apparently summer dwellings of this type were standard among many of the Eskimo until they were displaced by modern canvas tents late in the 19th century. The canvas tent shown in this scene is further evidence that the sketch was drawn in that period of Eskimo acculturation.

15 / Dragging a Seal Home. (Nat'-chik) Pencil, ink, and crayon; 5x8.

This Eskimo, dragging a small seal, is using the customary Eskimo method of carrying implements—in this case a rifle and a combination retrieving harpoon and ice pick.

This [retrieving] harpoon is used exclusively for retrieving seals that have been shot in open holes or leads of water within darting distance from the edge of the solid ice, and is thrown precisely as the walrus harpoon is, except that the end of the line is held in the left hand. In traveling over the ice the line with the head attached is folded in long hanks and slung on the gun case in the back. The rest of the weapon is carried in the hand and serves as a staff in walking and climbing over the ice, where the sharp pick is useful to prevent slipping and to try doubtful ice, and also enables the hunter to break away thin ice at the edge of the hole, so as to draw his game up to the solid floe. This peculiar form of harpoon is confined to the coast from Point Barrow to Bering Strait, the only region where the seal is hunted with the rifle in the small open holes of water.[28]

The use of a dragline for transporting game was another common Eskimo practice. In this sketch the artist may be implying that the Eskimo owns no dogs, or that he is unwilling to risk his dogs on unstable ice.

Encounters with bear

During the summer, when they ventured inland to search for caribou, the coastal Eskimo often encountered several species of bear.[29] The Meade River region, south of Point Barrow, has been described by several arctic authors as being well populated with bear, especially brown bear. Polar bears are not particularly common south of the Bering Strait, except at St. Lawrence Island. They seem to exist in greatest numbers in the Point Hope-Point Barrow region.[30]

References to the intentional hunting of bear in the interior seldom are found in arctic literature, but nearly all major writers and ethnographers of the arctic emphasize the struggles of the coastal Eskimo with the polar bear. There were several reasons for the Eskimo's encounters with the polar bear. Both were hunters of the seal, and, accidentally, they often came face to face in their search for that animal.

On occasions, the Eskimo sought to engage the polar bear. It was a dangerous act which brought considerable communal prestige. Also, the fur of the polar bear was a valuable commodity, especially suited for the making of mittens and boots. In recent decades the commercial value of polar bear skin has increased to the point where its importance to the arctic fur trade has endangered the existence of the species.

16 / **Bear Hunt** Lancing a bear, inland scene. Pencil, ink, and crayon; 4½x5¾.

17 / Lancing a polar bear, on the ice. Pencil and ink; 8x10.

18 / **Bear Hunt** Lancing a bear, inland scene. Pencil; 8x9.

19 / **Black Skin...** Hunting bear with a lance and bow and arrow. Pencil and watercolor; 8x9½.

20 / ... **Bear in the Water. (Ah'lik.)** Attacking a grizzly bear in the water. Pencil, ink, and crayon; 5x7¾ (fragmented).

Although these five scenes (16–20) emphasize reliance on native weapons (lance and bow), the Eskimo had guns in the period these sketches were produced. The hunters are shown using lances in sketches 16–18, but in the other two scenes they have been forced to rely on their double-curved, sinew-backed bow.

The situation depicted in sketch 20 seems fraught with danger, but the bear in sketch 19 seems resigned to his fate. The bear in sketch 20 is believed to represent a grizzly because the word "Ah'lik" in the artist's title probably is a variation of "aakluq," the Eskimo word for grizzly bear.[31]

40

17

18

19

20

POLARBEAR.

21 / A panorama of bear hunting. Pencil, ink, and crayon; 4¾x7¾.

This sketch depicts several series of events or various situations arising in encounters with bear. The bear in the top sequence appear to be polar bear (as indicated by the artist), but the color shading on the others may have been intended to represent brown bear, an inland species.

The top sequence emphasizes the role of dogs in the pursuit and dispatching of a polar bear. Of particular interest in this sequence are the design of the sled, harness arrangement of the dogs, use of the lance, and the Eskimo riding on the sled. All of these elements strongly suggest Siberian influence. The artist may have been familiar with St. Lawrence Island, where a number of such similarities also can be found.[32]

The bottom sequence seems to indicate a bow failure that resulted in use of a lance.

Encounters with lynx

22 / Running down a lynx. Pencil and watercolor; 8x9½.

23 / Running down a lynx. Pencil, ink and crayon; 5x7¾.

24 / Confrontation with a lynx. Pencil, ink, and crayon; 5x7¾.

25 / Returning with the kill. Pencil, ink, and crayon; 5x7¾.

The lynx was encountered in areas where the reindeer grazed and foxes were trapped.[33]

Together, these four scenes (22–25) depict a tale of pursuit, confrontation, and successful kill. It is unlikely that the lynx was hunted in the fashion suggested in these sketches. It is more probable that the encounter was an accidental one which afforded the particular Eskimo an opportunity to gain prestige[34] by proving his agility and endurance by "running" the lynx until it tired and then killing it with a mere stick.

Sketches 23–25 probably are the work of the same artist.

23

24

Trapping

The Eskimo used traps to capture such animals as the wolverine, fox, marmot (woodchuck), mink, and rabbit.

The wolverine's pelt, highly prized as decorative fur, was used for parka cuffs, tassels, and women's belts. In the arctic fur trade, the pelt of the wolverine was worth much more than that of many other furry animals.[35]

The pelt of the marmot was used principally for the making of summer clothes, so this animal usually was trapped in the spring.

Both the marmot and the mink were especially common at the head of Norton Sound and along the Seward Peninsula.

26 / Wolverine. (Kar've) Pursuing
an escaping wolverine. Pencil, ink,
and crayon; 5x7¾.

A trapped wolverine has managed to
pull loose the stake of a trap and is
on the verge of escape; but the Eskimo
trapper has arrived in time and will
try to kill the animal with a stick.

27 / Trapping Trapping marmots. Pencil and watercolor; 8x8¾.

An ethnographer's description of an Eskimo method of trapping marmots fits this sketch exactly:

> One method consists of a noose fastened to the end of a willow or alder stick 4 or 5 feet long, with the large end planted firmly in the snow or on the ground, the small end, having the noose attached to it, is bent down so that the noose hangs just over the marmot's runway in the ground, and is held in place by a small cross stick above it, which is hooked under a stick bent across the runway with its ends thrust into the ground. It is fastened so lightly that as the animal passes a touch releases the trigger and the bent stick springs up and catches it.[36]

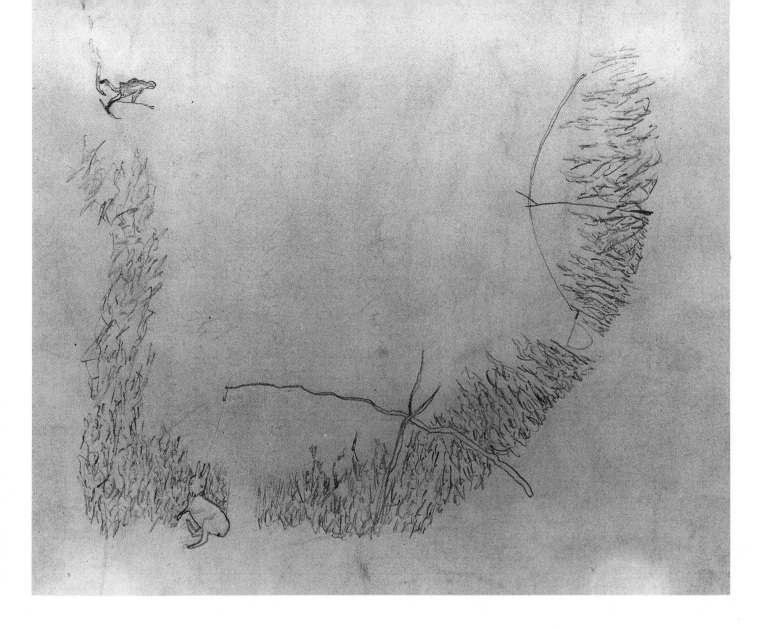

28 / Trapping Trapping rabbit.
Pencil; 8x9.

An arctic hare or white rabbit has
been caught in a snare set in an area
that the animal frequented—in the
brush or over a runway. The approaching Eskimo, on snowshoes, appears to
be carrying a forked stick which he
probably used when setting the snares.

29 / Returning from the Hunt
Hunters carry their quarry back to camp. Pencil; 8x9½.

This is a summer scene, as the men are lightly clothed and are not wearing snowshoes. Each is carrying two rabbits slung about his shoulders and held by a cord—a common method of transporting. One man carries a hatchet; the other a knife. Both carry a staff that could be either a walking stick or an instrument used in the setting of snares.

Caribou hunting

While they used caribou meat for food, the Eskimo valued the hide more than the meat. The hide was used in the manufacture and repair of winter clothing, and the skins of the fawn were valued over those of the adult caribou because of their lightness and lesser tendency to shed.[37]

30 / After the Hunt Camp of a caribou hunter. Pencil; 8x9.

Apparently the Eskimo in this scene is so far from the other hunters or the summer camp that he has decided to set up a temporary camp where he can butcher the meat and scrape and dry the hides. Normally, women would be summoned to a campsite to perform such work, so the men could continue their pursuit of caribou.[38]

The hunter is drying his boots and roasting some of the meat. Antler racks, hindquarters, hides, bow and arrows, and an equipment bag are in the foreground.

Otter and rabbit hunting

31 / Chasing a Land Otter in the Water   Pencil, ink, and crayon; 5x7¾

Two Eskimos in kayaks are pursuing a land otter that has taken to the water. Sharply pointed darts are being shot at the otter by means of an "atlatl" (throwing board). The darts are of the type normally used by the Eskimo in bird hunting. They are designed with opposing, excurvate bone points strategically placed along the shaft[39] in a manner which makes them especially effective when cast into a flock of birds. Since the Eskimos in this scene are equipped for bird hunting, it is possible that their encounter with the land otter was accidental.

The kayaks shown here are typical of those from the St. Michael area of Norton Sound.[40]

32 / Running down land otters. Pencil; 5x10.

33 / A Land Otter. (poom'cook-too)
Running down a land otter. Pencil and crayon; 4¾x7¾.

34 / Running down rabbits. Pencil and watercolor; 8x9.

Sometimes, hunting was a competitive event, with social implications. The successful hunter exhibited athletic prowess and endurance in running down certain animals. Since none of the quarry in sketches 32–34 had to be hunted in the manner shown, the hunters probably are engaging in athletic contests. Each scene shows two competitors.

The incident portrayed in sketch 32 appears to be taking place on the ice. The other two illustrations clearly are land scenes. In sketch 32 one of the hunters is wielding an ax to dispatch the quarry, probably a land otter. A spring scene is indicated in sketch 33. The vegetation and light clothing in sketch 34 imply a summer excursion.

33

34

Waterfowl hunting

Waterfowl, especially duck and geese, constituted an important secondary food supply for the coastal Eskimo. Often the hunters used snares, specially designed darts, and bolas to capture the birds. Along the arctic coasts the Eskimo designated particularly suitable bird-hunting stations where low-flying migrating birds could be brought down regularly, and often in large numbers. When the Eskimo made large kills they stored the excess supply in freeze cellars for future use.

During periods in the summer months when waterfowl could not fly because of molting, the Eskimo took full advantage of the situation and replenished his food stores to capacity. Ethnographers have noted the killing of molting waterfowl in the Yukon delta area, in the Point Barrow area and the region around the Meade River, and on sandbars of the Kukpuk River near Point Hope.[41]

The hunting of adult murres and the gathering of their eggs were annual summer events.

35 / Snaring Ducks   Pencil and pen; 6½ x 8.

This sketch depicts a technique that the Eskimo found effective in snaring ducks and other waterfowl. An ethnographer has described the kind of snare used in this method:

> It consists of a strong spruce root, three or four feet in length, with a rawhide cord fastened to each end, by which it is firmly attached to stakes. Spaced at regular intervals along this root are eight running nooses, also made of spruce root, spliced by one end to the main root, leaving a point projecting out about two inches, which serves to hold the noose open. The snares are set just above the surface of the water across the small openings in the floating grass and weeds, and as the birds attempt to pass through they are caught.[42]

Similarly constructed snares made of whalebone were obtained along the shores of Norton Sound and northward to Kowak River and Kotzebue Sound. Similar baleen loops have been recorded archeologically, suggesting that this method of snaring waterfowl had a long tradition among the Eskimo.

36 / Gathering Eggs from the Cliffs
Pencil, ink, and crayon; 9x12.

This realistically sketched scene shows an Eskimo gathering murre eggs from a rookery in ledges of the cliffs at Cape Thompson or Cape Lisburne.[43] The rigging being used here resembles the boatswain's chair used by seamen. The pole helped in negotiating the jagged rocks and was handy in dislodging the nesting murres.

Sometimes another method for gathering the eggs was used, but it was more dangerous. A seal net would be suspended from the top of the cliff and the hunter would scramble down to the ledges and put the eggs into a parka secured by a beltlike sash.

37 / Hunting Ducks Running down fowl in the molting season. Pencil and crayon; 8x9½.

The fowl depicted in this chase scene appear to be geese, which commonly were found molting in large numbers in regions around Point Barrow and the Meade River.

Fishing

Nine of the sketches (38–46) are devoted to arctic fishing, an important and dependable element of Eskimo economy the year round. A variety of fishing techniques were used.

During the summer salmon season numerous people from the interior and along the coast gathered at the best fishing locations. Even Eskimos who lived on the offshore islands came to the mainland for the salmon.

In the winter the Eskimo usually fished with individual lines through holes in the ice on the rivers, but they also used traps and weirs.

Many of the early ethnographers and Bureau of Education teachers became extremely interested in the unusual implements the Eskimo used in ice fishing, and a descriptive account by one of them is included in the discussion of sketch 38.

38 / Eskimo Fishing Fishing through the ice for sculpin. Pencil; 6½ x 9.

This Eskimo is fishing through the ice, probably for sculpin. Nearby are an ice pick and scoop fashioned from baleen.

For fishing through the ice a hole from six to eight inches in diameter is made. The ice pick employed for this purpose consists of a stout wooden staff, usually provided with a point made from the end of an old chisel or a flat piece of iron; but formerly, and indeed frequently during my residence in Alaska, picks pointed with reindeer horn or ivory were in use. . .

As the ice is generally several feet in thickness, the hole becomes filled with small fragments as the work of digging progresses. To remove these, as well as to skim out the film of ice that constantly forms on cold days, a small scoop with a netted bottom is used by the natives of the coast from the mouth of the Kuskokwim to Kotzebue sound.[44]

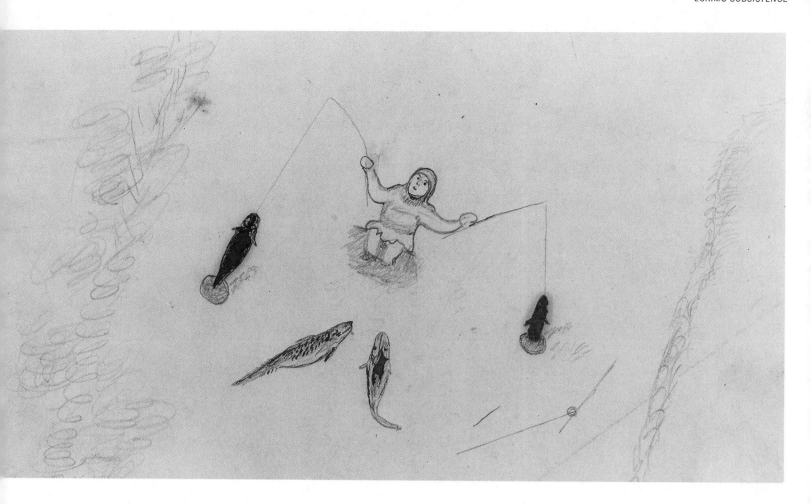

39 / Fishing in the Ice Pencil and ink; 5½ x 9¼ .

The Eskimo is fishing through two holes in the ice, obviously with great success. The artist apparently is telling his own ''fish story'' because the use of two fishing rigs through two holes would have been extremely difficult. The fish have some resemblance to cod, but there is not sufficient detail for positive identification.

40 / Fishing in the Ice   Pencil and ink; 7x9.

The fish in this scene resemble the northern pike but the artist, probably through oversight, has provided an extra dorsal fin not possessed by that species. The fisherman's available equipment includes the handy ice pick, baleen ice scoop, and other gear.

41 / Fishing through the ice for tomcod. Pencil, ink, and crayon; 5x7¾.

The sinker and hooks shown in this scene resemble types that have been attributed to St. Lawrence Island, but similar variations of these were in use along the coast of Norton Sound.[45]

As the weather warmed up in May, tomcod fishing began to pick up in Norton Sound, especially around St. Michael. The seaon continued through the fall, with the largest catches being made in November at St. Michael, through the ice.[46]

42 / Fishing through the ice. Pencil, ink, and crayon; 8x10.

In this sketch the Eskimo village in the background has certain characteristics which suggest that the scene is at Norton Sound.

The fish with two dorsal fins probably represent eulachon (candlefish); the others, smelt or grayling.

A Bureau of Education teacher has recorded a vivid account of the typical method of arctic ice fishing as sketched here:

This type of fishing [through the ice] is a two handed job, for two sticks, three feet long, one in either hand, are used. One stick has no line on it, and is used only to aid in hauling up the line. The actual fishing rod is strung from end to end with a strong, carefully made whalebone line, whalebone is the only primitive line that can be used. Any other material except wire would be covered with a new coat of ice every time it was pulled from the icy water into the frigid air, and the overlapping ice coats would soon break the line. Slush ice slips from the whalebone line just as it does from the guard hair of a polar bear emerging from the freezing sea.

The hook is made from discolored, fossilized beach ivory. . . . A short sharp pointed nail is put through the lower end and curved backward toward the line. The nail has no barb on it, so that when the line is pulled up, the fisherman can shake the fish off the hook without having to withdraw his hands from his mittens. The hook leaders are made from the quills of the goose and the crane, and from the tendons found in the legs of large birds. No bait is used, but sometimes fancy lures are fastened on the back of the hook.

When the nixie [here probably meant to be smelt] strikes, the pole is raised as quickly as possible. Simultaneously the stick in the other hand is pushed against the line near the ice, and by swinging the pole off to one side the line is drawn upward over the stick, thus lifting the fish clear of the fishing hole. When dropped on the ice, the fish wriggles free of the hook and is frozen stiff within a few seconds.[47]

43 / Fishing Fishing with traps and weirs. Pencil; 9x8.

Although this sketch lacks many details, it indicates the general technique of fishing with weirs and traps despite the handicap of ice: ''On the lower Yukon and Kuskokwim rivers wicker fish traps are set, with a brush and wicker work fence connecting them with the shore.'' [48]

In this scene, pliable net traps are being used instead of rigid wood traps.

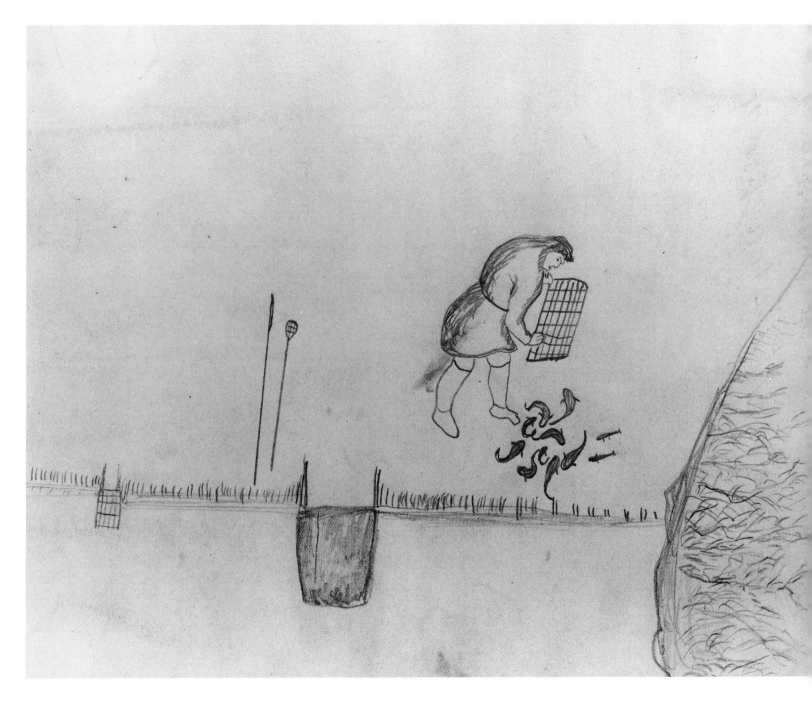

44 / Fishing Fishing with traps and weirs. Pencil; 6¾x8½.

The fish in this scene appear to be a mixed lot, possibly blackfish, burbot, and smelt. Few details of the trap's construction are shown.

The black fish is common wherever sluggish streams and lakelets occur from Kotzebue Sound to Kuskokwim River. Throughout this region they are taken by means of small wicker traps about 18 inches in diameter and 5 feet long, which are set in small streams, with a wicker fence leading from the mouths of the trap to the shore.[49]

45 / Seine Fishing Seining for salmon. Pencil, ink, and crayon; 6x9.

An Eskimo is having considerable success while seining for salmon with a gill net. Following is a description of this technique as used on the shores of Kotzebue Sound:

At Cape Blossom, on the arctic coast, the people were seen using gill nets about 25 feet in length, strung with floats and sinkers in the usual manner. A stout cord held one end fast to a stake on the shore, while the owner, by means of several slender poles lashed together, pushed the anchor stone on the other end out to its place, thus setting the net. When the floats gave indication that fish had been caught, the net was pulled in hand over hand, the fish removed, and the net reset.[50]

46 / Net Fishing Seining for salmon. Pencil, ink, and crayon; 6x9.

While this scene is similar to the one in sketch 45, the differences in hair style, clothing, and other details indicate it is the work of a different artist. The summer tent of modern design suggests the acculturation in the late 19th century.

Logging and wood gathering

47 / Logging with Dog Team
Artist, Stephan Ivanoff. Pencil and watercolor; 6¾x11¼.

The sizable stand of timber indicates that the scene is somewhere on the lower Yukon or near Unalakleet, where timber growth approaches the coast. The sled being used in the logging operation is a large "rail" type which, with some variation, was in common use from Point Barrow to Norton Sound.

The sketch bears the signature of Stephan Ivanoff and the lettering "Timbering W. 1892," and since another drawing (sketch 118) by the same artist is titled "Unalakleet River" it is possible that this timbering scene is on the eastern shore of Norton Sound.

Ivanoff, of Eskimo-Russian parentage and reared in the Unalakleet-Shaktolik area, eventually qualified, along with his wife, as a teaching assistant. By 1899 he was listed in the Alaska reports of the United States Bureau of Education as a native worker at the Swedish Evangelical Mission School at Unalakleet.[51] It is possible that in this scene the artist is portraying an activity which he witnessed or participated in while attending the Unalakleet school in 1892.

48 / Dog-Sledding Transporting a load of wood. Pencil, ink, and crayon; 8x10.

A rail sled is heavily laden with what appears to be sawed lumber. Evidently the artist was portraying a purely fictional event, as there are only three sled dogs and the Eskimo has added his own weight to the already massive load. The preceding and following sketches depict essentially the same activity but they show considerably more detail.

49 / Drawing Wood with Dog Sleds
Pencil and watercolor; 8x10.

In this panorama the artist has depicted the Eskimo village in a curious fashion, with one enormous building among a number of small dwellings. The large house probably is the "kashim," a community house large enough to hold most of the village population for social events and to serve through the winter as a "lodge" for the men of the village.

This particular kashim has a flat roof and other features not typically characteristic of arctic Eskimo construction. It may represent a type of structure that developed in the acculturation process so pronounced during the 1890s. Old photographs of Shishmaref village on the Seward Peninsula between Cape Espenburg and Cape Prince of Wales show acculturated structures which, in the summer, appear to be partially unsodded, such as the kashim in this scene.[52]

Storing provisions

50 / Caching provisions on an elevated platform. Pencil, ink, and crayon; 4¼ x 5¾.

The Eskimos are hoisting a provision-packed sled onto a platform where it will be cached. The raised platform protected the often irreplaceable food reserves from marauding animals as well as from the ever-present, always-hungry, village dogs. When extremely hungry, Eskimo dogs were known to devour even the lashings on sleds.

The Eskimo house has a ground-level, covered entranceway of a type commonly found in the Norton Sound region.[53] In the winter such houses were entered through an underground passageway which prevented the loss of interior heat. In summer, the ground-level entrance was used, and the tunnel served as a food cellar.

51 / Filling Skin-Bottles with Berries and Oil   Ink and crayon; 7¼ x 9½.

Seal skins, with the hair removed, are being filled with a mixture of berries and oil, a preserve which the Eskimo considered a delicacy and saved for use in winter or on special occasions.
In autumn the women gather a large supply of blue berries, heath berries, salmon berries, and cran berries, which they store for winter use. At this season is also gathered a kind of sorrel, which is boiled and crushed with a pestle and then put into a wooden tub or barrel and covered with water where it is left to ferment in the sun. This makes a very pleasant acid relish, which is added to various dishes in the winter and is called ko-pa-tuk.[54]

Eskimo transportation

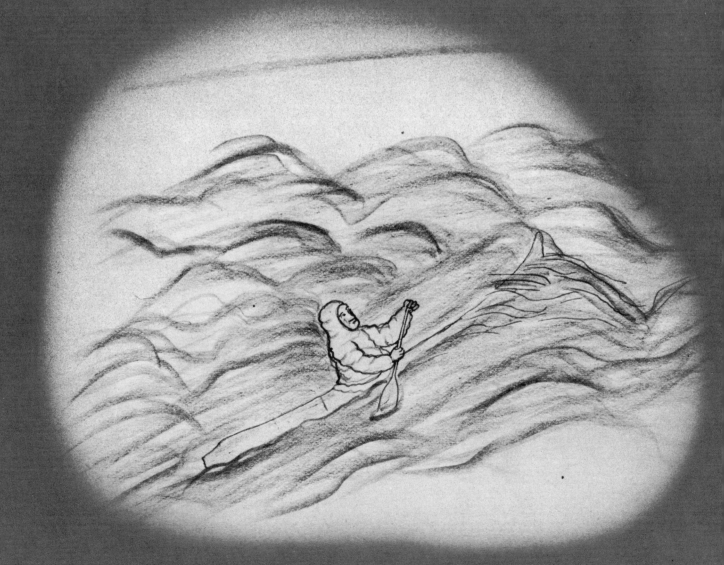

When they planned to build such a boat they would select two long "menikke," heavy logs, which had the proper upturn at the root end. These were then shaped to the proper thickness and spliced together at the straight ends. For this splicing seal skin thongs were used. In this manner the keel of the boat was laid; to this was fastened thin ribs at the approximate spacings of four feet apart. These ribs were as high as the boat should be when completed. To the tops of these ribs were tied two inch thick railings. To cover the ribs of the boat they used walrus skins. The hide of the walrus is very thick and may be split two or three times. The outer or hair side, with the hair scraped off, was used for the boat covering. They would let it lie soaking in water for several days. Then they sewed three or four skins together and stretched this covering loosely across the frame of the boat, and as the skins dried they would draw up as tight as the frame of the boat could stand. These boats were watertight until they had been several days in the water. In the bottom, at least, they would place boards so as not to step through the bottom.[55]

Seats, paddles, and a sail were than added to complete the umiak.

Umiaks had far less variation in construction than the kayaks, which can be identified as to provenance on the basis of their structural details.

52 / Hauling-up an umiak Pencil and crayon; 4¾x7¾.

In this summer scene nine Eskimos are transporting an umiak to higher ground. The features and costumes of the individuals have been carefully drawn. The single vertical tattoo on the woman's chin implys she is youthful.[56] There seems to be a suggestion of conversation between the two men standing near the umiak's bow. Possibly the man in the ankle-length parka is greeting some new arrivals to a summer encampment. The canvas tent nearby verifies that the season is summer.

The kayak

Like the umiak, the kayak was constructed of easily replaceable and repairable materials. The design allowed for protection in severe weather, yet the boat was so light it could be handled with minimum effort in or out of the water.

The rim of the kayak's manhole is made slightly flaring or with the cover constricted just beneath it next to the deck. Around this constriction a cord is passed, which fastens down the borders of the waterproof frock worn by the occupant in rough or wet weather. With this garment lashed down it is impossible for any water to reach the interior.[57]

53 / Paddling a kayak in heavy seas. Pencil, ink, and crayon; 5x7¾.

An Eskimo traveler is encountering very rough weather while trying to maneuver his kayak amidst cakes of drifting ice. He is wearing a ''gut'' type of frock which, in effect, is part of the kayak.

The kayak's structural design indicates the scene may be on Kotzebue Sound.[58]

54 / Norton Sound kayaks. Pencil;
6¼ x 8¾.

Three kayaks are underway, possibly
in pursuit of some prey, as a variety
of harpoons or darts are bracketed
to the hulls. This scene could also
portray a competitive event, especially
since there are minor structural variations in the design of the kayaks.

All three kayaks can be attributed
to the Norton Sound region, with the
top and middle boats probably from
the vicinity of St. Michael.[59]

Dog sledding

55 / Through the Ice   The dangers of travel on ice. Pencil, ink, and crayon; 5x7¾.

In the arctic, the old, thick ice nearest shore usually is relatively stable and can be traveled upon. Beyond, the young ice can break away from the old ice in large masses and then, when currents and winds combine, suddenly move toward the shoreline, ultimately crashing into the old ice and endangering anyone or anything caught in the open water. New ice, which forms nearest the edge of the young ice or between the young and old ice, is the most dangerous for travel because it is thin.

While out on the ice the Eskimo had to be constantly attentive to noises, winds, and currents that might hint of impending danger. He had to be ever watchful for open-water "leads" that might close, carefully listen for sounds of folding ice, and always be aware of the possibility that the ice mass he was traversing could drift out to sea.

This drawing, more than any other in the collection, demonstrates the atmosphere of danger that constantly surrounded the Eskimo during his daily activities. Incidents like the one depicted in this scene—where a laden sled has fallen through the ice—were commonplace but never to be taken casually. A man could be partially submerged for a brief period, but he would have to extricate himself before his clothing became saturated and porous. Following such a dunking the Eskimo would have to remove the quickly formed ice on the surface of his drenched clothing. Fortunately, in this scene there are two men, and one has been able to maintain his footing on an unbroken part of the ice.

The design of the boat being hauled is partially obscured, but judging from the stern construction it is a kayak of the type from the St. Michael area of Norton Sound.[60]

56 / A reluctant dog team. Pencil, ink, and crayon; 4¾x7¾.

Teams of from five to nine dogs were standard for pulling loaded sleds. Although it is conceivable that the three dogs shown here could pull the load, before long they would show the fatigue the artist has indicated.

Details of the sled's construction identify a type that was used by the Malamute Eskimo in the vicinity of St. Michael, Norton Sound.[61]

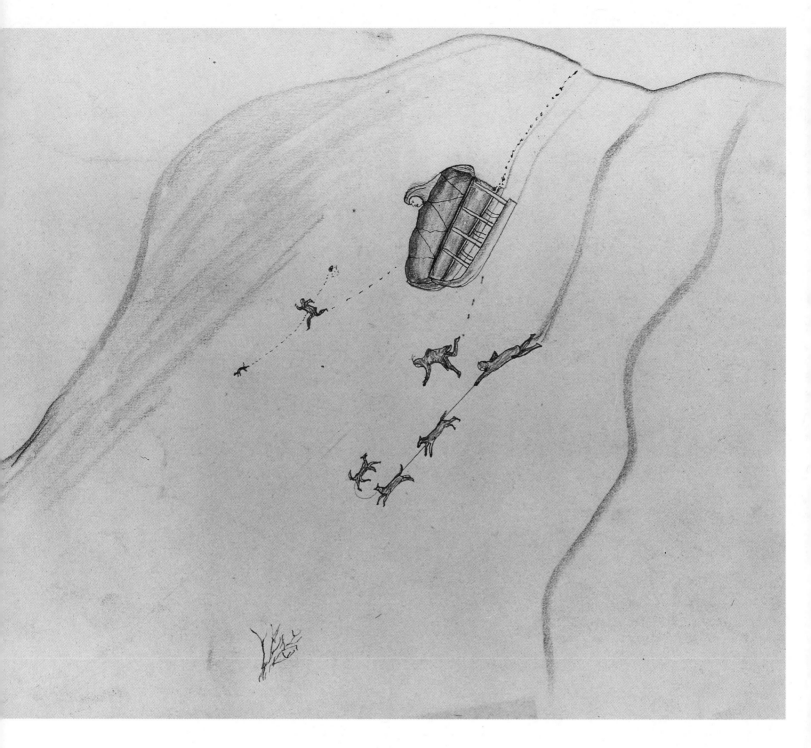

57 / A runaway dog team. Pencil and ink; 8x10.

Despite the artist's unsuccessful attempt at perspective, the story behind this scene is quite exciting. Apparently a small animal, possibly a fox, had darted from its den on the slope of a hill just as the loaded dog sled was approaching. The resulting commotion of this accidental encounter is apparent.

One of the Eskimos, obviously quite upset, is in pursuit of the villain while two others are desperately trying to recover the dog team. If the grade of the slope is as steep as it appears to be, the Eskimo on the sled is about to experience the ride of his life. Perhaps the artist had once been involved in a similar incident and was recalling the details of his experience.

58 / Dog sledding. Pencil, ink, and crayon; fragment, 6¼ x 10.

The sprinting Eskimo in this scene shows that the dog team is making good time despite the heavily laden sled.

Packing

59 / An Eskimo woman "packing" an animal. Pencil and ink; 8x10.

The Eskimo woman is transporting a reindeer fawn or a dog and is leading a dog by a leash. She may be returning a fawn that had become separated from the herd or unable to keep up with it.

60 / Packing over the Mountain
Pencil and ink; 8x9¼ .

An Eskimo family is packing over a
steep mountain. The man is heavily
burdened, probably with a tent and
skins, and he carries a lance which
doubles as a staff. The woman is
carrying a large bag, perhaps contain-
ing utensils and food, and a small box
that might contain trinkets. The child
is apparently too small to carry anything. The dog, probably a favorite,
is heavily loaded with additional stores
or trading material. Although all Eskimo dogs were burden animals, some
dogs were favorites and were treated
like pets.

*Considerable care is bestowed on
the puppies. Those born in the winter are frequently reared in the iglu,
and the women often carry a young
puppy around in the jacket as they
would a child.*[62]

Trade

Although an appreciable amount of merchandise flowed between the Eskimo and interior Indian groups, most arctic trade was between the various coastal peoples on both sides of the Bering Strait:

In ancient times intertribal communication along the coast was irregular and uncertain, owing to the hostile attitude of the people toward one another. For this reason trading was then confined to those villages which happened to be on friendly terms. Now [1877–1881] the old barriers have been broken down, and active barter between the different communities has become a marked feature of their life. This is particularly the case among the people living between the Kuskokwim and Kotzebue sound. The numerous fur-trading stations which have been established among them, and the visits of trading vessels and whaling ships to the coast of Bering strait, have served to quicken and encourage among them the spirit of trade. In summer the people of Bering strait make visits to the head of Kotzebue sound and to the mouth of the Yukon, carrying the skins of tame reindeer purchased from the people of the Asiatic coast, for which they received in barter skins of various fur-bearing animals that are used in turn for trading with vessels in Bering strait or with their Asiatic neighbors. For the latter purpose beaver and land-otter skins are the most highly prized, as the Chukchi of Siberia will always offer two full-size deerskins for one of either of the skins named. They cut them into strips for trimming the collars of their deerskin coats, and use them also for trading with Russians.

Parties of traders from East cape, Siberia and the Diomede islands also make yearly voyages to Kotzebue sound, where the Eskimo of Kowak and Noatak rivers hold a sort of summer fair. After the sea freezes in winter, the Eskimo, who have thus obtained a stock of reindeer skins, start out with dogs and sledges to travel along the coast and barter for furs. . . .

During trading voyages there are carried from one part of the country to another beads and other articles of use or ornament, as well as pieces of jadeite. . . . Small articles, such as green and red paint and wooden dishes, were sent out from the lower Yukon; and the people of other localities who have a surplus of seal oil, dried fish, and skins of various animals, take them to points where they can be exchanged for other desirable commodities.[63]

The following remarks describe the manner of trade between the Eskimo and Indians in the Kotzebue Sound region:

The Kobuk [Eskimo] traded caribou hides, parkas, and seal oil and blubber, obtained from coast peoples, for skins of beaver, fox, mink, mountain sheep, weasel, and wolverine, and such articles of clothing as moccasins, decorated shirts, and beaded mittens. At the conclusion of the trading, which might last almost throughout the summer, the Indian visitors invited the Kobuk to their village for reciprocal feasting and trading. The Kobuk always visited the Indians in late winter or in spring, rather than in summer.

The Kobuk not only traded with the Indians, but many in summer went to Sheshalik on the coast for fishing and beluga hunting. Then they visited Kotzebue for feasting and trading, receiving seal-skins and seal blubber and oil in return for the pelts of inland animals. In late fall they returned to their own village.[64]

The bartering scenes depicted in sketches 61–63 concern the proposed exchange of the ever-valuable wolverine pelt for several marmot or fox pelts. The commodity in sketch 64 cannot be identified.

Since "tupeks," or summer dwellings, appear in two of these sketches, it is possible that these scenes refer to the summer trade fair that was held each summer on the shores of Hotham Inlet on Kotzebue Sound. There, trade items from as far away as Siberia and the offshore islands as well as local goods were bartered and purchased for use in the coming winter. This annual mixing of peoples is reflected in the different kinds of clothing the participants are wearing.

61 / Barter Fur trading in summer.
Pencil and watercolor; 6¼ x 9.

The traders resemble the typical
coastal Eskimo as represented in most
of the drawings in the collection.

62 / Barter   Fur trading in summer.
Pencil and watercolor; 7¾x9.

The man on the right is wearing a cap
which is not unlike a type of leather
headgear worn by the Kobuk Eskimo
in the vicinity of Hotham Inlet.

63 / Barter Fur trading in summer.
Pencil and watercolor; 4½ x 8¾.

The participants in this scene do not
have the appearance of Eskimo.

64 / Barter Summer trading. Pencil ink, and crayon; 8x10.

The couples in this scene probably are Eskimo and Indian.

Conflicts 65 / **A Fight** Pencil and ink; 5x7¾.

In addition to the drawn knives the combatants have clasped their free hands, further evidence of the gravity of the quarrel. Situations such as this were not uncommon, and sometimes they led to long-standing family feuds. Often the causes for such feuds were trivial: "two men disagree over the ownership of a duck shot while hunting and one kills the other." [65] Here, the artist is indicating that the wolverine is the subject of the dispute.

98

66, 67 / A Duel Pencil; 4x6¾ and 3¾x8½.

These sequential scenes depict the progress of a duel. Apparently the two combatants are exchanging alternate shots from their bows. In both sketches the figures at lower right probably represent the causes of the duels. In sketch 67 the faintly outlined figure seems to be that of a woman.

The combatants' bows are of the typical Eskimo reflex or sinew-backed type, but the costumes are suggestive of an interior people, possibly Athabascan Indians.

The following account of an Eskimo duel would fit the situation sketched in these two scenes:

After a time, Kayaakpuq, discovering the affair, got his bow and attempted to kill his rival. Tiguaceak, however, was warned by his relatives and carried his own bow. The two men exchanged a volley of arrows but each missed the other. When this duel occurred, Kallikcuk left her husband and went to live in the house of Tiguaceak as his second wife. . . .

It so happened that the family of Kallikcuk sided with the former husband. One of her brothers came each day to stand guard over Kayaakpuq. One day, Tiguaceak came, an arrow fitted to his bow. Kallikcuk's brother walked toward him. Each man had a reserve of about 20 arrows. These they discharged from a distance. At length, Tiguaceak succeeded in hitting his opponent in the upper arm. The wounded man came back to where Kayaakuq was standing. Kallikcuk's father was present and came forward to assist his wounded son. He drew the arrow from the wound, remarking to Kayaakpuq: "Unless you go after him now, you'll always be afraid of him." Kayaakpuq did not reply but took his former brother-in-law's bow and remaining arrows and went out, walking slowly through the houses toward Tiguaceak. The latter came out again and exchanged arrows with him. At last an arrow shot by Kayaakpuq struck Tiguaceak in the ear and he fell dead.[66]

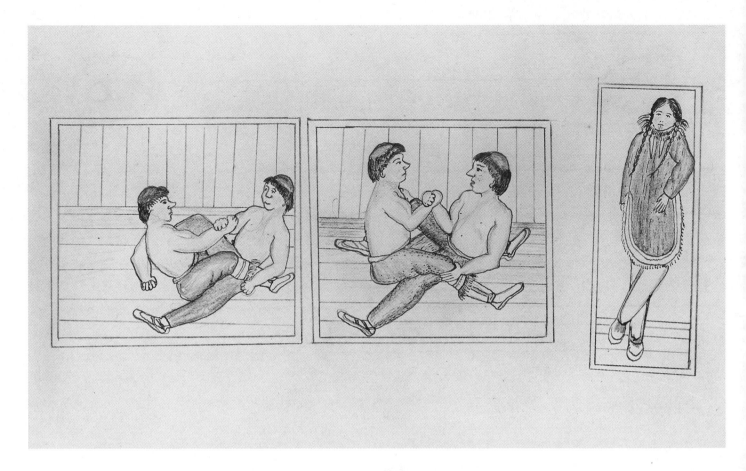

Wrestling

68 / Wrestling in the kashim. Pencil and ink.

These scenes may be interpreted in several ways. First, the nonchalant stance of the Eskimo woman while a wrestling bout is in progress would suggest that the women became quite bored during the winter season when the men remained for long periods in the village kashim engaging in continuous sports. A second possibility is that the scene is applicable to a comment by an ethnographer that wrestling "is generally done for sport, but . . . in ancient times disputed claims for women were sometimes settled in this manner." [67] If the latter interpretation is the correct one, the Eskimo woman certainly seems unconcerned about the outcome.

69 / Wrestling contests in the kashim.
Pencil and crayon; 4¾x7¾.

The competition shown in these three wrestling matches is a variation of the "finger pull." Each wrestler is clutching a small wooden or bone cylinder that is connected by a line to another such cylinder. The contestants are at right angles to each other, and the objective appears to be either to break the arm brace of the opponent or pull him over.

Some of the other competitive events that took place in the kashim were arm pulling, stick raising, foot pulling, and head pushing.[68] As a result of these strenuous events, the Eskimo men were able to maintain a degree of physical fitness despite the severity of the weather during the winter months.

The color of the clothing of one of the wrestlers is the same in each match, while that of his opponents varys. By this treatment the artist probably is indicating that one man is the champion and the others are challengers. The drawings in the triangles at the top and bottom of the scenes are unique in the collection.

Football

The following five sketches depict a favorite pastime of the coastal Eskimo—football or, more precisely, kickball. The origin of this sport among the coastal Eskimo is uncertain, but it probably resulted from contact with non-Eskimo populations.

It has been noted that Eskimo football games were held both north and south of St. Michael, Norton Sound, during the years 1877–1881.[69] The more-sophisticated forms of Eskimo football were common in the St. Michael area, where goals, boundaries, and designated player assignments seem to indicate that the game originated there some time in the second half of the 19th century.

During the 1890s, due in part to large numbers of marooned whalers, several marathon football games took place in the arctic.

Towards the end of the 19th century when large numbers of the inland Eskimo (Noatarmiut and Kovagmiut), together with the Tigara men, were recruited by American whalers to hunt whales each spring, there was a large temporary camp of natives at a place called Jabbertown on the Point Hope bar, 6 miles east of Tigara. Each spring during that period a great football game was played by the Tikerarmiut men and the men from the interior. The inland people kicked towards the mainland and the Tikerarmiut towards the Point. The playing field extended 10 or 12 miles along the bar. The game continued for several days. Sometimes it resulted in bitter fights and broken heads.[70]

One of the first and probably the best known of the land-based commercial whalers in the arctic recorded the following comments on Eskimo football as it was played near Point Barrow:

As played by the Eskimo, football was a game of endurance, not skill. Every moonlit night, spring and fall, the whole village turned out for the sport, and . . . we'd all been joining in. The ball used was about eight inches in diameter and covered with tanned deerskin, each side kicking it along the hard snow. Since there were no goals nor any limit to the playing field, a game might end five or six miles from the start.

The great game of 1895 was certainly the longest and best that had taken place. It ended as usual far out on the sea ice amid holes already melted large enough for setting seal nets.[71]

Details of the game as it was played at St. Michael have been recorded by an ethnographer:

I saw it played in various places from Bering strait to the mouth of the Kuskokwim; at Cape Darby it was played by children on the hard, drifted snow; it is also a popular game on the lower Yukon. Two of the participants act as leaders, one on each side choosing a player alternately from among those gathered until they are equally divided. At a given distance apart two conspicuous marks are made on the snow or ground which serve as goals, the players stand each by their goal and the ball is tossed upon the ground midway between them; a rush is then made, each side striving to drive the ball across its adversaries' line.

Another football game is begun by the men standing in two close, parallel lines midway between the goals, their legs and bodies forming two walls. The ball is then thrown between them and driven back and forth by kicks and blows until it passes through one of the lines; as soon as this occurs all rush to drive it to one or the other of the goals.[72]

The same author has described the game as it was played by women in the St. Michael area, usually in the fall and winter:

The ball used is generally considerably larger than the one used in the men's game. The four players stand opposite each other [in four positions resembling the major points of the compass]. . . .

Each pair has a ball, which is thrown or driven back and forth across the square. The ball is thrown upon the ground midway between the players, so that it shall bound toward the opposite one. She strikes the ball down and back toward her partner with the palm of her open hand. Sometimes the ball is caught on the toe or hand and tossed up and struck or kicked back toward the other side. The person who misses least or has fewer "dead" balls on her side wins. At times this game is played by only two women.[73]

Four of the following five scenes show both men and women participating. In several of the scenes the enthusiasm of the players is particularly evident. Some of the men are shown sporting a belt to which an animal's tail is attached:

Attached to the belt are various amulets and at the back always the tail of an animal, usually a wolverine's. Very seldom a wolf's tail is worn, but nearly all, even the boys, have wolverine tails, which are always saved for this purpose and used for no other.[74]

70 / Football Pencil and ink,
4¾ x 7¾ .

71 / Game of Ball Pencil and ink,
8 x 10.

72 / Ball Game Pencil and ink,
7½ x 11.

73 / Game of Ball Pencil and ink,
8 x 10.

74 / Game of Ball Pencil, ink, and
crayon, 8 x 10.

71

72

73

74

Ceremonials

The Messenger Feast (depicted in sketches 75–83) was the greatest of the Eskimo socioceremonial holidays, usually taking place in December or January. There were many variations on the basic theme, both geographically and temporally, which account for the differences presented in the literature. A description of the feast as it was conducted at Point Barrow (1881–1883) contains various details that can be noted in several of the sketches:

> After all had finished [activity outside the kashim] as many as
> could get in entered the "dance house." At one end of this a
> small space was partitioned off with a piece of an old sail. . . .
> Presently the bottom of the curtain was lifted and out crawled
> five men on all fours, wearing on their heads the stuffed skins
> of the heads of different animals—the wolf, bear, fox, lynx, and
> dog. They swung their heads from side to side in unison, keeping time to the music, uttering a low growl at each swing and
> shaking their rattle mittens.[75]

Kotzebue Sound is another locale where details of the Messenger Feast have been described:

> The origin legend of the Kotzebue Messenger Feast (Kotzebue
> is approximately 200 miles south of Pt. Barrow) states that wolf-
> head masks were worn, presumbly made of real headskin, and
> that stuffed animal heads, birdskins, decorated drums, carved
> objects, sealskins and eagle feathers were hung in the Kashim.
> This was definitely a Messenger Feast: two messengers, each
> carrying marked staffs, formally invited the guest villages.[76]

75 / A preliminary event outside the kashim during the Messenger Feast. Pencil, ink, and crayon; 5x7¾.

This sketch pictures one of the initial events of the multiple-day Messenger Feast:

> *Eskimo celebrated their Christmas by first reenacting their "ipanee" [old time] dance. They always spend several weeks making the necessary preparations to give this great exhibition. . . . They started it off by dividing the people into two companies. Each side chose a young man, to whose forehead they fastened perpendicularly a single arctic owl wing or tail feather. The two chosen youths ran a foot race to decide which side should perform first. After the race, the winning side took up its position about fifty feet from and facing the defeated side, and while they beat their sowyits [drums] on the underside with long, thin, flexible sticks, they sang the song of victory to the losers. . . . When they finished [Woman's chant], old Ahtanak [a particular Eskimo] appeared dressed in a singular headgear of feathers, with a loon head protruding from his forehead. He was jumping hilariously, carrying a blazing torch on the end of a long pole.*[77]

The scene clearly shows the two groups of participants, those with the sleds being the "invited." All are gathered around the entrance to the kashim, the house where most of the events will take place. The blazing torch, or wand, was used as a sort of baton carried by the "messenger."

76 / At a Mask-Dance Pencil, ink, and crayon; 8x10.

77 / Events within the kashim. Pencil, ink, and crayon; 5x7¾.

78 / At a Mask-Dance Pencil and watercolor; 8x10.

79 / Events within the kashim. Pencil and ink; 4¾x7¾.

80 / At a Dance Pencil, ink, and crayon; 8x10.

81 / At a dance. Pencil, ink, and crayon; 4¾x7¾.

82 / At a Mask-Dance Pencil and ink; 6½x10.

83 / At a Mask-Dance Pencil, ink, and crayon; 8x10.

Sketches 76–83 focus on events of the Messenger Feast that took place within the kashim.

The spectators and sowyit (drum) players were seated on one side of the room, on the floor; the women stood on the opposite side next to the wall, each holding a stick with a bunch of gull or owl feathers fastened to the end, with which they beat time to the music. Directly in front of them were the performers wearing feather headgear and big seal gauntlet gloves, trimmed with trinkets which jingled with every movement of the hands.

Kotook, the oomalik [chief] drummer, beat upon a wooden pack-ing case [formerly a box drum] with a handle fastened to the side of it, which was suspended from the ceiling on a sealskin rope, in the middle of the room . . . at intervals he [the drummer] passed sticks of wood behind him, which Anyih [a particular Eskimo] took, representing presents to the other side.[78]

In several scenes some of the figures appear unfinished, a treatment which may have been the artist's method of enhancing perspective and focusing attention upon the central figures.

Sketches 76 and 77 depict the same dance scene, as viewed from the dancers toward the drummers and spectators. In sketch 76, the legs of the dancers are schematized. The cir-

77

cular hole in the floor near the box drum is the entrance to the kashim's main chamber. The drummer's baton probably is a piece of carved ivory.

On the American shore of Bering strait, and thence northward along the arctic coast, resonant pieces of wood are regularly beaten to aid the drum accompaniment during dancing. For this purpose a short, heavy baton of walrus ivory is generally used. Such an instrument was obtained at Port Clarence. It is 10½ inches in length. . . . On its outer end the mouth, eyes and blow holes of a right whale are represented by incised holes and pits. Between the blow holes are inserted some small, downy feathers, held in place by wooden pegs, to represent the spouting of the whale.[79]

In sketch 78 the women participants are standing on a sleeping-platform typically found in most Eskimo dwellings but usually reserved for male members of the family and guests. The women are holding feather wands and are attired in what is probably their finest apparel. In front of the women

are five men also arrayed in fine garments, who are sitting on the same platform. On the floor of the kashim, in front of the other participants, are five dancers wearing elaborate costumes with feather headdresses and "puffin-beak," gauntlet-type mittens, a type particularly common in the Norton Sound area. Behind the dancers and below the platform is a partition or screen with multiple openings. The use of the partition is shown in greater detail in subsequent scenes.

Sketches 79 and 80 provide similar views but with minor changes of detail, such as the interior timbers of the kashim and stuffed birds high on the walls—a Kotzebue custom. In sketch 80 the box-shaped object on the floor of the kashim is probably a token gift for the invited who have come to the Messenger Feast.

Sketch 81 provides a view over the backs of the drummers toward the partitioned area. Four masked figures are shown with their heads and mittened arms protruding through openings in the partition.

In sketch 82 the events of the previ-

ous scene have progressed, and the masked dancers are now being ministered to by the performers on the platform. The animal heads probably are intended to represent wolves. The women with their feather wands have been drawn in a slanting fashion that may be suggestive of a weaving or chanting posture.

In the final dance scene (sketch 83), the "wolf" dancers have come forth from the partition onto the open floor of the kashim and, while sitting, are making rythmic motions. The figures sitting on the platform are still ministering to the dancers. Several nude figures on the platform are displaying rather menacing expressions.

79

80

81

82

83

84 / A Race   A preliminary event in a ceremonial. Pencil and crayon; 8x10.

The fancy garments of the racers and the small objects held in their hands suggest that this contest is part of a ceremony. Several Eskimo feasts began with a footrace which determined the order of performance and participation in the ceremonial.[80] At the end of the whaling season a feast called the "nalukataq" was held to celebrate the successes of the season, and races also were held during this feast.[81] It may be only coincidental, but the small objects held by the contestants in this scene resemble the tail of a whale.

85 / Winter activity in the kashim.
Pencil, ink, and crayon; 6¼ x 10.

This scene, within a kashim, depicts four Eskimos about to engage in some kind of social activity. Each man is holding a pole-like instrument which resembles a whaling spade or a broom. These men possibly are participating in a ceremony related to whaling. The dark circular area in the foreground is the entrance to the kashim.

Mythology 86 / An Eskimo myth. Pencil, ink, and crayon. 8x10.

This sketch depicts a large birdlike creature carrying off a bowhead whale. The scene probably is a pictographic rendition of an Eskimo myth:

Tin-mi-uk-puk, *the great eagle [Thunderbird]. This is described as an enormous eagle which varies in its habits according to locality. The people of the Bering Strait said that it preys upon right whales. . . . On the shore of Norton Sound the* Tin-mi-uk-puk *is said to catch either whales or reindeer (caribou) and along the lower Yukon it was reported to prey upon people and reindeer (caribou).*[82]

Reindeer in
Alaska

Introduction of the reindeer

One man who attempted to protect the Alaskan Eskimo against the destructive aspects of acculturation was Dr. Sheldon Jackson. As "General Agent of Education for Alaska" he made several journeys, particularly in 1890, to the homeland of his charges and keenly observed their way of life. With this background he found it necessary to look beyond the basic concern—education—and focus on supplementation of the fading Eskimo economy. In reporting on his trips to Alaska, Jackson repeatedly commented on the precariously unstable subsistence pattern of Eskimo life.

From time immemorial they [the Eskimo] have lived upon the whale, the walrus, and the seal of their coasts, the fish and aquatic birds of their rivers, and the caribou or wild reindeer of their coast inland plains.

The supply of these in years past was abundant and furnished ample food for all the people . . . as the great herds of buffalo that once roamed the western prairies have been exterminated for their pelts, so the whales have been sacrificed for the fat that encased their bodies and the bone that hung in their mouths. . . . But commerce wanted more ivory, and the whalers turned their attention to the walrus, destroying thousands annually for the sake of their tusks. . . .

The seal and sea lion, once so common in the Bering Sea, are now becoming scarce. . . . With the advent of improved breach-loading firearms the wild reindeer (caribou) are both being killed off and frightened away to the remote and more inaccessible regions of the interior and another source of food supply is diminishing. Thus the support of the people is largely gone and the process of slow starvation and extermination has commenced along the whole arctic coast of Alaska. . . .

In this crisis it is important that steps should be taken at once to afford relief. Relief can, of course, be afforded by Congress voting an appropriation to feed them, as it has done for so many of the North American Indians. But I think it may not be necessary to extend that system to the Eskimo of Alaska. It would cost hundreds of thousands of dollars annually, and worse than that, degrade, pauperize, and finally exterminate the people. There is a better, cheaper, and more practical, and more humane way, and that is to introduce into northern Alaska the domesticated reindeer of Siberia, and train the Eskimo young men in the management, care and propagation.[83]

Dr. Jackson began his project to bolster the Eskimo economy in 1891. He instigated the transportation of a number of reindeer from Siberia across the Bering Sea to Amaknak and Unalaska islands in the Aleutian chain. These "trial" animals survived the voyage of 1,000 miles, wintered well, and were in good condition in the spring of 1892. In the autumn a bill was introduced in the Senate ap-

propriating $15,000, to be spent under the direction of the Secretary of the Interior, for introducing and maintaining reindeer in the territory of Alaska for domestic purposes.[84]

The first northern Alaskan reindeer station was established in 1892 near the entrance to Norton Sound at Port Clarence. During the fair weather season five trips were made to Siberia and a total of four Siberian (Chuckchee) herdsmen were obtained to initially manage the herds with the assistance of a few Alaskan Eskimo apprentices.[85]

The Chuckchee herders were soon replaced with Norwegian Laplanders to train the Eskimo as herdsmen. To the Eskimo and others the Lapps became known as the "card people," for their tricornered hats and colorful costumes resembled those of the "kings" and "jacks" of playing cards.

Between 1891 and 1902 more than 1,200 reindeer were landed at the main reindeer station at Teller, a short distance from Port Clarence. The new herds were dispersed both north and south. Although there were the expected setbacks, by 1914 the reindeer industry was sufficiently prosperous to attract outside interests.

Invariably, when the whaling season began, the reindeer herds near the coasts where the whales passed received little or no attention for long periods. The herders simply preferred to hunt whale. On the other hand, reindeer herding was easily adopted into the culture of interior Eskimo groups which traditionally practiced a migratory subsistence closely tied to the movements of the caribou herds. Some coastal Eskimo groups that were less dependent on sea mammals also found reindeer herding a boon to their economy.

As part of their assignment, the teachers employed by the Bureau of Education were called upon to supervise the maintenance of local Eskimo reindeer herds. This added responsibility required numerous long journeys into the interior, in all kinds of weather, to inspect the herds, bring provisions, pay the herders, and annually assist in the roundup, division, and counting.

Although some contemporary ethnohistorians feel that the reindeer industry was predestined to failure for various reasons, some Bureau of Education teachers expressed a different view:

It is difficult to conceive how the Eskimo could get along without this new, apparently indispensable animal. The entire deer is utilized for one purpose or another. The principal clothing of the Eskimos and certainly the warmest they wear is made from reindeer skin (formerly caribou). Skins from the legs of two deer makes the uppers for their warmest winter *kumiks (boots)*. The meat is sweet, juicy, and tender; steaks can be cut with a fork, and, fried in their own fat, they are delicious. The blood is saved, frozen in vessels, and chunks of it are dropped into soup and dog food. The marrow bones are cracked and boiled, and the fat is used in the mixture dubbed "Eskimo ice cream".... A

slab of sinew taken from the back makes the Eskimo their strong-
est and best thread. Rims for ice hole fishing scoops are made
from the antlers, also knife handles, dog harness swivels, and
even bows for boy archers.[86]

The Eskimos have been severely censured by their critics, the
corporations and other nonnative owners, charging that they do
not have good appliances and do not care for their herds. Con-
sidering that they did not have other than what they earned by
their wages in reindeer or other manner, while the corporations
boast of millions of dollars invested, the native has done remarkably well, and until the heresy of "open herding" was introduced, and his deer were mixed with the white men's herds, to
his loss and damage, he has accomplished much for a man
only one lifetime removed from a hunter on the sea.[87]

*An outgrowth of the reindeer industry was the use of reindeer as
beasts of burden.*

Since the Siberian natives have used the reindeer for transport
and since the Lapps have successfully broken the reindeer to
the sled, this animal, feeding itself on tundra moss as it does,
was conceptually ideal for Alaskan native life. Superficially, the
idea seems excellent; the carnivorous dog, which makes such
heavy inroads on the human food supply, could successfully be
replaced.[88]

But the replacing of dogs by reindeer had certain disadvantages.

. . . while deer may be better for traveling in the interior, where
moss is so plentiful that no food need be carried for them, yet in
traveling along the coast, a dog team is much preferable. Deer
tire quickly and have to eat frequently. Dogs will haul a much
heavier load than the two hundred pounds that is a maximum
load for a deer. Deer are bothered by dogs. Moss being scarce near
the beach, the deer have to be driven far inland from the villages
to be fed; whereas with dogs the traveler can pitch anywhere as
long as he has dried fish, or seal or whale meat on the sled for
them. Dogs are tougher and will travel much farther. We have
driven our dog teams seventy miles a day with a load.[89]

87 / Teller Reindeer Station
Pencil, ink, and crayon; 7 ¼ x 10.

This scene is at the first reindeer station, located at Port Clarence on the
south shore of Seward Peninsula. The
grazing herd is accompanied by two
herdsmen. Fawns, which can be seen
among the herd, usually were born
some time after the middle of April.

88 / Reindeer Farm Reindeer in the fawning season. Pencil, ink, and crayon; 7½ x10.

During the fawning season the herd was much more vulnerable to roving predators, especially wolves. When the fawning season happened to coincide with the spring whaling season the herds sometimes were left unattended and suffered severe losses.

A teacher and reindeer supervisor for the Bureau of Education has summarized the duties and rewards of a typical Eskimo reindeer herder:

At the expiration of four years training, an apprentice becomes a full-fledged herder. For his services he is rewarded by the Reindeer Department of the United States Board of Education as follows: First year: ten reindeer and $150 worth of groceries, ammunition, traps, tents, dry goods, etc. Second year: eight deer and $100 in supplies. Third year: six deer and $75 in supplies. Fourth year: same as third. By this time his herd is supposed to number fifty deer; and when it numbers one hundred, he is expected to take and train his first apprentice. When it numbers 150, he takes another apprentice, and so on, until he has trained four apprentices.[90]

89 / **Laplanders Camp**   Pencil, ink, and crayon; 5x7¾.

A Lapp family is portrayed in front of its dwellings. The Laplanders are in typical costume, including tricornered hats, shoes with pointed, upturned toes, a dagger, and garments with colorful trimmings.

90 / Laplander camp and reindeer herd. Pencil, ink, and crayon; 5x7¾.

Two Lapps are shown gathering wood in this panorama of a camp and reindeer herd.

91 / Herding Reindeer Pencil and crayon; 5x7¾.

In this spring scene the Lapp herder has his reindeer on the move.

92 / "My friend the reindeer." Pencil,
ink, and crayon; 5x7¾.

The artist's message here is obvious—
friendship, or more realistically, the
feeling by the Eskimo that the reindeer, if cared for properly, provided
economic security. This particular
sketch certainly would have been useful as publicity during the early days
of the Alaskan reindeer industry, as it
clearly expresses one Eskimo's senti-
ment in regard to the introduction of
reindeer to his land. In any event, the
artist has captured a charming scene
of sensitivity.

130

Reindeer sledding

Some of the scenes in the following series of sketches depict the Siberian type of sled, suggesting that the artists had been exposed to the Siberian Chuckchee herders imported into Alaska during the early years of the reindeer industry. With the rising curved runners and particularly light construction of the Siberian sleds, it is not surprising that the Eskimo preferred them to the heavy-duty, coastal-Eskimo type of sled. The rail sled of the interior Eskimo was also more suitable to reindeer usage and it, too, became standard reindeer equipment. Combining a light Siberian sled and a medium-weight Alaskan rail sled apparently offered certain advantages, and this arrangement is shown in several scenes.

93 / Breaking reindeer to the sled. Pencil and crayon; 5x7¾.

Two Eskimos are trying to break deer to the sled, but apparently with limited success.

Reindeer are driven with a single line of walrus rope or window-sash cord—which also serves two other purposes, being a lasso and grazing line. . . . They are driven like a dog team by calling "gee" and "haw"; they are generally broken to respond to the single line hitting them on the sides, right side for "gee" and left for "haw." They are very contrary; to drive them is sometimes very much like driving a hog. Until they got well broken in, we never knew which direction they were going to take.

It was very amusing to watch the boys [Eskimos] break sled deer. Some deer would get vicious; they would stand on their hind feet and with their sharp hoofs strike terrific blows at the drivers, who were very careful not to get hit. They would start off like a shot. The driver would make a lunge for the sled, perhaps miss it, land in the snow, and be dragged a short distance. The neck of a deer is not as strong as that of a horse, so he is turned around in a semicircle (by the driver holding on the line) and brought to a stop. Then the driver makes a leap for the sled again; this time he may light on it at right angles, and before he can get seated, the deer may cut a circle and send him and the sled rolling over and over.[91]

94, 95 / Reindeer Sledding Pencil, ink, and crayon; 9x12 and 9x11½.

In these sketches a harness-racing or touch-type whip is being used, and the reindeer are effectively harnessed.

96 / Reindeer Sledding Pencil, ink and crayon; 7½ x 10.

The driver is using a dog-team type whip, and the reindeer is too far from the sled to be controllable. Perhaps the artist is pointing out the awkwardness of an early attempt at reindeer sledding when the correct method was not understood and the influence of dog sledding still dominated.

97 / Reindeer. (Kon'nah.)   Pencil,
ink, and crayon; 5x7¾.

98 / Reindeer Sledding   Pencil and
ink; 6½x7¾.

Sketches 97 and 98 depict what was
probably the accepted and most ef-
ficient technique of harnessing and
controlling the animals. The ends of
the harness reins are looped around
the drivers' wrists, allowing freedom
to apply the whip without dropping
the reins.

98

99 / Harnessing Reindeer Pencil
and ink; 7¼ x 10.

In this scene only one reindeer is
harnessed, and one wonders whether
the artist is implying a slight degree
of complacency on the part of the
reindeer.

100, 101 / Domestic Reindeer
Harnessed reindeer. Pencil and ink;
6½ x 7½ and 6½ x 8¼ .

The harness shown in sketch 100 appears to be very efficiently designed. It probably was issued by the United States government.

102 / Reindeer Sledding   A reindeer pack train. Pencil and ink; 6½x8¼ .

Stores are being hauled by reindeer harnessed in tandem, or single alignment. For dog sledding, the animals usually were aligned in pairs. In this scene a Siberian-type sled is being used in conjunction with the more typical Eskimo rail sled.

103 / A reindeer hauling a boat. Pencil and crayon; 4¾x7¾.

Transportation has come to a halt, and the Eskimo appears to be encouraging the reindeer to resume his work.

104 / Taking a Canoe Over-Land
Pencil, ink, and crayon; 5½ x 10.

Four reindeer are hauling an umiak and a kayak. The stern design of the kayak is typical of craft used in the region of Norton Sound.

105 / Using reindeer for transportation. Pencil and crayon; 4¾x7¾.

The Eskimo probably are moving the herd of reindeer to a better grazing area, usually farther inland.

Nature studies

106 / An ermine. Pencil, 8x9.

The ermine is shown near some unidentifiable vegetation.

107 / A weasel. Pencil, 8x8¾.

The animal either is outside its own
den or is poaching the den of a prey.

108 / A red fox. Pencil and crayon; 8x10.

The Eskimo believed that the red fox possessed exceptional capabilities:
It was the red fox which was regarded as the most cunning of all the animals. The red fox can approach close to humans, knowing that his intelligence will keep him safe, and it is the red fox which will avoid a trap. It takes a resourceful hunter to get the red fox.[92]

109 / Reindeer or caribou. Pencil
and watercolor; 8x10.

110 / Reindeer or caribou. Pencil,
ink, and crayon; 8x7½ .

111 / Reindeer or caribou. Pencil
and watercolor; 7¼ x10.

112 / Two bucks lock horns. Pencil,
6½ x10.

In sketches 109–112, depicting reindeer or caribou, styles of several artists
are apparent in the different treatment
of the figures.
    Combats such as the one portrayed
in sketch 112 could be fatal to both
animals if the horns became inextri-
cably locked.

111

152

112

113 / A wolf attacking a reindeer or caribou. Pencil and ink; 6¼ x 9.

The animal's throat, the most vulnerable spot, is the focus of the wolf's lunge. Normally a wolf would not engage a reindeer or caribou of this size unless the animal was crippled or very old. Fawns and dogs were less dangerous prey.

114 / Walrus on drifting ice. Pencil, ink, and crayon; 4¾x7¾.

Walrus are quite menacing with their long tusks and are formidable in size, but their diet is principally clams, which they gather by using their tusks as picks or rakes. Like the reindeer, the walrus has the curious ability to separate food from residue entirely within its mouth and then discard the nonedibles.

115 / Arctic hare. Pencil; 8x9.

The impression of distortion in this sketch may be the result of an ineffective attempt at perspective. On the other hand, the artist may have been trying for a stylized, three-dimensional effect, and implying that the hare is alert to the danger of an approaching hunter despite the distance between them.

It is rather unlikely that this scene is related to an Eskimo myth such as that of the "dwarf people." [93]

Landscapes

116 / Village scene. Pencil; 5¾x9¼

This scene may have been drawn by the same artist who depicted the village shown in sketch 49. Certain details correspond—the oversize kashim, smaller buildings, and elevated caches.

The smaller elements, mostly in the foreground, probably represent stacks of wood that were used as grave coverings. Because of the permafrost, the dead often were placed directly on the frozen ground or in boxes and then covered with driftwood or whale ribs to protect against predators.

Stephan Ivanoff.

U. R.

117 / U. R. Unalaklik River. Artist, Stephan Ivanoff; colored pencil and watercolor; 6¾ x 10½ .

118 / **Unalaklik River, 1892** Artist,
Stephan Ivanoff; ink and watercolor;
6¾x9½

119, 120 / Koko Creek   Artist, Stephan Ivanoff; pencil, ink, and watercolor; 5½ x 8⅛ and 5¾ x 11¾.

The sparsely vegetated hillsides in these sketches suggest that these scenes are northwest of Unalaklik in the western part of Seward Peninsula. However, several Eskimo villages on the lower Yukon River have similar names—for example, "Koko" and "Kokok."

Stephan Ivanoff   Laho Creek

References

Andrews, Clarence L. *The Eskimo and His Reindeer in Alaska.* Caldwell, Idaho: Caxton Printers, Ltd., 1939.

Annual Reports of the Bureau of Education for the years 1891–1892, 1892–1893, 1899–1900, and 1903. Washington, D.C.

Baker, Marcus. *Geographic Dictionary of Alaska.* (Bulletin of the United States Geological Survey, No. 187.) Washington: 1901.

Brower, Charles D. *Fifty Years Below Zero.* New York: Dodd, Mead and Company, 1942.

Curtis, E. S. *The North American Indian.* Volume 20. Norwood, Massachusetts: Plimpton Press, 1930.

Hoffman, Walter J. "The Graphic Art of the Eskimos." *Report of the U.S. National Museum . . . for the Year Ending June 30, 1895,* pages 739–968. Washington: Government Printing Office, 1897.

Johnshoy, J. W. *Apaurak in Alaska.* Philadelphia: Dorrance and Company, 1944.

Keithahn, E. L. *Eskimo Adventure.* Seattle: Superior Publishing Company, 1963.

Lantis, Margaret. *Alaskan Eskimo Ceremonialism.* American Ethnological Society. New York: J. J. Augustin, 1947.

Murdock, John. "Ethnological Results of the Point Barrow Expedition." *Ninth Annual Report of the Bureau of American Ethnology . . . 1887–'88,* pages 19–441. Washington: U. S. Government Printing Office, 1892.

Nelson, E. W. "The Eskimo about Bering Strait." *Eighteenth Annual Report of the Bureau of American Ethnology . . . 1896–97,* part 1, pages 19–518. Washington: U. S. Government Printing Office, 1899.

Rainey, F. G. "The Whale Hunters of Tigara." *Anthropological Papers of the American Museum of Natural History,* volume 41, part 2, pages 231–283.

Ray, Dorothy. *Artists of the Tundra and the Sea.* Seattle: University of Washington Press.

—————. "Alaskan Eskimo Arts and Crafts." *The Beaver,* autumn 1967, pages 80–91.

Spencer, R. F. *The Northern Alaskan Eskimo: A Study in Ecology and Society.* (Bureau of American Ethnology Bulletin 171.) Washington: Smithsonian Institution, 1959.

Vanstone, James W. *Point Hope, An Eskimo Village in Transition.* Seattle: University of Washington Press, 1962.

Van Valin, W. B. *Eskimoland Speaks.* Caldwell, Idaho: Caxton Printers, Ltd., 1941.

Notes

1. USNM history card for accession number 51115.
2. NMNH ethnology catalog card number 260447.
3. NMNH ethnology catalog card number 260882.
4. Baker, page 249.
5. NMNH ethnology catalog card number 260790.
6. Baker, page 401.
7. *Annual Report of the U. S. Bureau of Education for the Year 1903,* volume 2, page 2354.
8. *Annual Report of the U. S. Bureau of Education for the Year 1899–1900,* volume 2, page 1749.
9. Ray, "Alaska Eskimo Arts and Crafts," page 84.
10. Ray, *Artists of the Tundra and the Sea,* figure 58.
11. NMNH ethnology catalog card number 168997.
12. *New York Herald,* 24 October 1909.
13. *The New York Times,* 11 January 1937.
14. *Annual Report of the U. S. Bureau of Education: for the Year 1889–90,* pages 1254–1257; *for the Year 1899–1900,* pages 1744–1747; *for the Year 1905,* pages 276–277.
15. *Annual Report of the U. S. Bureau of Education for the Year 1899–1900,* page 1674. Also, NMNH ethnology photo number 13793.
16. *Annual Report of the U. S. Bureau of Education for the Year 1891–92,* page 874.
17. Vanstone, page 20.
18. Vanstone, page 24.
19. Vanstone, page 24.
20. Brower, page 124.
21. Brower, page 139.
22. Murdock, pages 187–188.
23. Vanstone, page 49.
24. Van Valin, page 169.
25. Nelson, page 220 and plate 79.
26. NMNH ethnology specimen number 44449.
27. Nelson, page 260.
28. Murdock, pages 230–231.
29. Rainey, pages 266–267.
30. Nelson, page 120.
31. Spencer, page 32.
32. Nelson, page 208 and figure 62.
33. Andrews, page 142.
34. Nelson, page 119.
35. Nelson, page 232.
36. Nelson, page 124.
37. Rainey, page 266.
38. Rainey, page 267.
39. Nelson, plates 53 and 59.
40. Nelson, plates 53 and 58. Also NMNH ethnology specimen numbers 129325 and 368250.

41. Nelson, page 135. Also, Rainey, page 267.
42. Nelson, page 134.
43. Rainey, page 266.
44. Nelson, pages 174–175.
45. Nelson, page 176 and plate 68.
46. Nelson, pages 174, 176.
47. Van Valin, pages 101–102.
48. Nelson, pages 184–184 and plate 71.
49. Nelson, page 184.
50. Nelson, pages 185–186.
51. *Annual Report of the U. S. Bureau of Education for the Year 1899–1900,* page 1750.
52. Keithahn, page 30.
53. Murdock, page 78.
54. Nelson, page 268.
55. Johnshoy, pages 85–86.
56. Murdock, pages 138–139.
57. Nelson, page 221.
58. Nelson, page 221 and plate 79.
59. Nelson, page 220 and plate 79.
60. Nelson, page 220 and plate 79.
61. Nelson, page 205 and plate 75.
62. Murdock, page 358.
63. Nelson, pages 229–230.
64. Curtis, page 214.
65. Rainey, page 242.
66. Spencer, pages 118–119.
67. Nelson, page 340.
68. Nelson, page 339.
69. Nelson, page 335.
70. Rainey, pages 256–257.
71. Brower, page 175.
72. Nelson, pages 335–336.
73. Nelson, page 336.
74. Murdock, page 138.
75. Murdock, page 374.
76. Lantis, page 70.
77. Van Valin, pages 53–54.
78. Van Valin, pages 55–56.
79. Nelson, pages 352–353 and figure 138.
80. Spencer, pages 219–220.
81. Spencer, pages 350–352.
82. Nelson, pages 445–446.
83. *Annual Report of the U. S. Bureau of Education for the Year 1889–1890,* pages 1291–1292.
84. *Annual Report of the U. S. Bureau of Education for the Year 1892–93,* pages 1707–1708.
85. *Annual Report of the U. S. Bureau of Education for the Year 1892–93,* page 1708.

86. Van Valin, page 70.
87. Andrews, pages 145–146.
88. Spencer, page 365.
89. Van Valin, pages 69–70.
90. Van Valin, page 64.
91. Van Valin, pages 68–69.
92. Spencer, page 267.
93. Nelson, pages 480–481.